SOCIAL MEDIA FOR SMALL BUSINESSES

Engaging Your Audience

DAVID M ARNOLD

Crystal Coast HR

Social Media

This Page is Blank

Disclaimer

The content provided in *Social Media for Small Businesses* is for informational and educational purposes only. The strategies, tips, and advice shared are based on general social media marketing principles and are intended to help small business owners enhance their online presence. However, the effectiveness of these strategies may vary based on individual circumstances, market conditions, and platform algorithms, which are subject to change.

This guide does not guarantee specific results, such as increased followers, engagement, or sales, and should not be considered as professional marketing, legal, or financial advice. Readers are encouraged to conduct their own research, adapt strategies to fit their unique business needs, and consult with a professional marketing expert if necessary.

By using this guide, you agree that the author and publisher shall not be held liable for any losses, damages, or negative outcomes resulting from the application of the information provided. Use this content at your own discretion.

Copyright

Acknowledgments

I am deeply grateful to everyone who has supported me in the creation of *Social Media for Small Businesses*. This book would not have been possible without the encouragement, guidance, and inspiration from many individuals along the way.

First and foremost, I want to thank my family for their unwavering support, patience, and understanding during the long hours of writing and research. Your love and encouragement have been my greatest source of motivation.

A special thank you to my colleagues and clients at Crystal Coast HR, Crystal Coast Websites, and EBL Training. Your insights, experiences, and challenges have greatly influenced the content of this book. Your dedication to growing small businesses has been a continual source of inspiration.

Lastly, to all the small business owners, entrepreneurs, and marketers who are striving to make their mark in the digital world—this book is for you. I hope it serves as a valuable resource in your journey toward social media success.

Thank you all for your support, trust, and encouragement.

Dedication

To Paula—your unwavering love, encouragement, and patience have been my greatest source of strength.

To the small business owners and entrepreneurs who dare to dream big and face the challenges of growing their businesses in a constantly evolving digital world—this book is dedicated to you.

May it serve as a guide, a source of inspiration, and a tool to help you succeed on your journey.

And to God, whose wisdom and grace guide me in all that I do—this work is a testament to the blessings you have bestowed upon me.

Table of Contents

Social Media

Preface

In today's digital age, social media has transformed the way we connect, communicate, and do business. What started as a means to stay in touch with friends and family has evolved into a powerful marketing platform that offers brands the opportunity to engage with audiences on a global scale. Whether you're a small business owner, a marketing professional, or an entrepreneur looking to grow your brand, mastering social media is no longer a luxury—it's a necessity.

The challenge, however, lies in navigating the ever-changing social media landscape. New platforms, algorithm updates, shifting consumer preferences, and emerging trends can make it difficult to keep up. Many businesses struggle to break through the noise, build meaningful connections, and convert followers into loyal customers. This guide was created to help you overcome those challenges.

The purpose of this guide is to provide you with a clear, actionable roadmap to social media success. We've distilled years of social media marketing experience into practical strategies, tips, and best practices that you can apply immediately. Whether you're just starting out or looking to refine your existing strategy, this guide covers everything from understanding your audience and creating compelling content to leveraging advanced tools and analyzing your performance.

But more than just a how-to manual, this guide emphasizes the principles of consistency, authenticity, and engagement— the three pillars of social media success. These core principles are what set apart the brands that thrive from those that merely survive in the digital space. By applying these concepts to your social media strategy, you'll be able to build a strong online presence that not only attracts followers but also fosters genuine connections and drives real business results.

As you embark on this journey, remember that social media is as much about people as it is about platforms. It's about creating value, fostering relationships, and building a community that believes in your brand. The insights shared in this guide are designed to empower you to leverage social media in a way that aligns with your brand's unique voice, goals, and vision.

We hope that this guide not only equips you with the tools you need to succeed but also inspires you to see social media as a dynamic and exciting avenue for growth. The journey may require effort, experimentation, and a willingness to adapt, but the rewards are well worth it.

So, let's get started. Together, we'll explore the strategies, techniques, and opportunities that will help you harness the full potential of social media, and turn your digital presence into a powerful force for your brand. Welcome to the world of social media mastery—your guide to creating, connecting, and thriving online.

Introduction

Social media has fundamentally transformed the way businesses interact with their customers, market their products, and build brand loyalty. For small businesses, social media is more than just a platform for socializing; it's a powerful tool for growth and engagement. The good news? You don't need a massive marketing budget or a dedicated social media team to succeed. With the right strategies, even the smallest business can leverage social media to reach new audiences, boost customer loyalty, and drive sales. That's the purpose of this eBook, *Social Media for Small Businesses: A Step-by-Step Guide to Engaging Your Audience*. Whether you're a beginner or a seasoned entrepreneur looking to refine your social media strategy, this guide is packed with practical tips, actionable insights, and step-by-step instructions to help you achieve your social media goals.

Purpose of the eBook

In today's digital age, having a strong social media presence is no longer optional—it's essential. The purpose of this eBook is to empower small business owners like you with the knowledge and tools to master social media marketing. We know that running a small business is a balancing act, and adding social media to the mix can feel overwhelming. That's why this guide is designed to simplify the process, breaking down complex concepts into easy-to-understand strategies that you can implement immediately.

Here's what you'll gain from reading this eBook:

- **Clear Strategies for Social Media Success**: Understand the ins and outs of major platforms like Facebook, Instagram, and LinkedIn, and how to use them to your advantage.

- **Actionable Tips**: Each chapter is filled with practical advice that you can apply to your business right away.

- **Tools and Resources**: From content calendars to analytics tools, this guide includes everything you need to manage your social media accounts effectively.

- **Scalable Solutions**: Whether you're just starting out or looking to grow your online presence, the strategies in this book are scalable to fit businesses of all sizes.

By the end of this eBook, you'll have a solid social media strategy that not only increases your brand's visibility but also drives engagement and sales.

Why Social Media Matters for Small Businesses

The impact of social media on consumer behavior is undeniable. Here are some key statistics to consider:

- **Over 4.7 billion people** use social media globally, spending an average of **2 hours and 30 minutes** daily on various platforms.

- **73% of marketers** believe that social media marketing has been "somewhat effective" or "very effective" for their business.

- **50% of consumers** report that they are more likely to buy from a brand they follow on social media.

These numbers aren't just statistics—they're opportunities. By tapping into the power of social media, you can:

- **Increase Brand Awareness**: Reach a wider audience and build a recognizable brand.

- **Drive Customer Engagement**: Foster direct communication with your customers, answering their questions, addressing their concerns, and building loyalty.

- **Generate Leads and Sales**: Use social media as a cost-effective way to drive traffic to your website, generate leads, and convert followers into customers.

- **Gain Valuable Insights**: Social media analytics provide valuable data on your audience's preferences, behaviors, and engagement patterns, allowing you to refine your marketing strategies.

Benefits of an Active Social Media Presence:

1. **Enhanced Brand Visibility**: Social media allows you to showcase your brand's personality, values, and products in a way that's engaging and relatable.

2. **Improved Customer Trust**: Regular interaction with your audience builds trust and credibility, especially when you provide valuable content and responsive customer service.

3. **Cost-Effective Advertising**: Social media advertising is significantly more cost-effective than traditional forms of advertising, making it accessible even to small businesses with limited budgets.

4. **Real-Time Feedback**: Use social media as a platform to get instant feedback from your customers, helping you improve your products, services, and overall customer experience.

5. **Competitive Edge**: A well-executed social media strategy can set you apart from competitors, especially if they're not as active or strategic on social platforms.

Who This Guide Is For

This eBook is designed for a wide range of readers, including:

- **Small Business Owners**: If you're running a local shop, restaurant, online store, or service-based business, you'll find strategies to help you grow your online presence and connect with customers.

- **Entrepreneurs and Startups**: Launching a new business? This guide will help you build a social media presence from scratch and create buzz around your brand.

- **Marketing Professionals**: If you're responsible for managing social media channels, this guide offers tips to optimize your campaigns and increase ROI.

- **Social Media Managers**: Whether you're working in-house or as a freelancer, you'll find advanced strategies to boost engagement, grow followers, and measure the success of your efforts.

This eBook is structured to provide practical advice and real-world examples that you can adapt to your specific business needs, making it an invaluable resource for anyone looking to master social media marketing.

How to Use This eBook

Social media is constantly evolving, with new features, algorithms, and best practices emerging regularly. To help you stay ahead of the curve, this eBook is structured in a step-by-step format that makes it easy to follow and implement. Here's how to get the most out of this guide:

1. **Step-by-Step Approach**: The eBook is organized into chapters that build upon each other, covering everything from setting up your social media profiles to creating engaging content and measuring your success.

2. **Practical Examples**: Throughout the guide, you'll find real-life case studies and examples of small businesses that have successfully leveraged social media to achieve their goals.

3. **Actionable Tips and Checklists**: Each chapter concludes with actionable tips and checklists to help you put what you've learned into practice.

4. **Templates and Resources**: To save you time, we've included templates for social media calendars, content creation, and performance tracking, which you can customize to fit your business.

5. **Interactive Exercises**: At the end of certain chapters, you'll find exercises designed to help you apply the concepts and strategies you've learned.

6. **Scalable Strategies**: Whether you're just starting out or looking to scale your social media efforts, the strategies outlined in this guide are flexible enough to accommodate your unique business goals and resources.

What You'll Learn:

- How to choose the right social media platforms for your business.

- Proven strategies for creating high-quality content that resonates with your audience.

- Techniques for growing your followers organically and through paid advertising.

- Tools for scheduling, managing, and analyzing your social media campaigns.

- Best practices for engaging with your audience and turning followers into loyal customers.

Your Social Media Journey Starts Here

Social media is not just a trend; it's a vital part of modern business strategy. As a small business owner, the question is no longer **if** you should be on social media, but **how** you can leverage it effectively. This eBook is your guide to mastering social media, helping you navigate the challenges and maximize the opportunities available to your business.

So, are you ready to unlock the full potential of social media for your business? Let's get started and turn your social media channels into powerful marketing tools that drive real results.

Chapter 1: Getting Started with Social Media

Social media can be a game-changer for small businesses, but diving into it without a clear plan can lead to wasted time, effort, and resources. The good news? With the right approach, social media can help you achieve your business goals, connect with your audience, and even drive sales. This chapter will guide you through the foundational steps of getting started on social media, from setting clear goals to choosing the right platforms and creating a winning strategy.

Defining Your Social Media Goals

Before you create your first post or launch a campaign, it's critical to define what you want to achieve with social media. Without clear goals, you risk wasting time and resources on efforts that don't align with your overall business strategy. A well-defined goal gives you a clear direction and purpose, helping you stay focused, measure your success, and make necessary adjustments. Let's explore common social media goals for small businesses and how to set them effectively.

Common Goals for Small Businesses

1. Brand Awareness

One of the most popular reasons businesses use social media is to increase their brand visibility. Social media allows businesses to reach a wider audience, making their brand more recognizable and creating opportunities for word-of-mouth marketing. By consistently sharing high-quality, engaging content, you can establish your brand's identity and attract new followers who are interested in what you offer.

> **Example:** A local bakery could use Instagram to showcase mouth-watering photos of their latest pastries, creating an irresistible visual appeal. By sharing customer reviews and behind-the-scenes stories, the bakery can build a connection with food lovers in the area and attract potential customers.

2. Lead Generation

Social media is a powerful tool for capturing leads. By using targeted strategies such as sharing helpful content, running contests, or utilizing paid advertisements, businesses can encourage users to provide their contact details (like email addresses), which can later be nurtured into customers. Generating leads via social media can help small businesses grow their customer base without the need for expensive marketing campaigns.

> **Example:** A software company might offer a free eBook or downloadable guide in exchange for email sign-ups on LinkedIn. Once users provide their email addresses, the

company can send them targeted content and eventually convert these leads into paying customers.

3. **Customer Support**

In today's digital landscape, customers expect quick and easy access to support. Social media has become a primary channel for businesses to address customer queries, resolve concerns, and provide exceptional service. Offering timely responses to issues raised on platforms like Facebook, Twitter, or Instagram not only enhances customer satisfaction but also builds brand loyalty. A proactive customer service presence on social media can help businesses stand out from the competition.

> **Example:** An online clothing store could use Twitter to address customer questions about shipping times, returns, or product availability. By responding quickly and effectively, the brand can foster a positive relationship with customers and create an image of reliability.

4. **Community Building**

Social media allows businesses to foster a sense of community by engaging with their audience, sharing valuable content, and facilitating two-way communication. Building a loyal online community is especially important for businesses that rely on repeat customers, brand ambassadors, and word-of-mouth referrals. When your audience feels connected to your brand, they are more likely to become repeat customers and recommend your products or services to others.

> **Example:** A fitness studio could create a private Facebook group where members can interact, share workout tips, and celebrate personal achievements. This sense of belonging strengthens the relationship

between the brand and its customers, encouraging continued engagement and loyalty.

How to Set SMART Social Media Goals

To ensure that your social media efforts are aligned with your business objectives, it's essential to set SMART goals—goals that are **Specific, Measurable, Achievable, Relevant**, and **Time-bound**. This framework helps you stay focused, track progress, and ultimately measure success.

1. Specific

Your goal should be clear and focused. Instead of setting a vague goal like "increase followers," aim for something more precise. This makes it easier to stay on track and understand when you've successfully achieved your goal.

> **Example**: "Gain 1,000 new Instagram followers in 3 months" is much more specific than just wanting to increase followers.

2. Measurable

Ensure that your goal can be tracked and measured using data. Use social media analytics tools (such as those built into platforms like Facebook Insights or Instagram Analytics) to monitor your progress. Metrics like engagement rates, click-through rates, and conversion rates can help you assess whether you're on target.

> **Example**: "Increase website traffic by 20% over the next quarter through targeted social media ads" is a measurable goal that allows you to track progress using website analytics tools like Google Analytics.

3. Achievable

Your goals should be realistic and attainable given your current resources, capabilities, and time. While it's great to set ambitious targets, avoid aiming for goals that are too far out of reach, as this could lead to frustration and disappointment.

> **Example**: If your business is just starting out, aiming for 100,000 followers within a month might not be achievable. Instead, focus on steady, incremental growth, like gaining 500 followers within the first month, which you can then build upon.

4. Relevant

Your social media goals should align with your overall business objectives. Make sure that your goals are relevant to your business's current needs and growth stages. If your priority is to grow brand awareness, focus on creating content that amplifies your visibility. If you want to increase sales, create goals that focus on lead generation and conversions.

> **Example**: If your primary goal is to grow your email list for an upcoming product launch, your social media goals should include capturing leads through forms, sign-ups, or giveaways.

5. Time-bound

Set a clear deadline for achieving your goal. Having a timeframe creates a sense of urgency and helps you stay focused. It also allows you to assess the effectiveness of your strategies and make adjustments if necessary.

> **Example**: "Increase website traffic by 15% within the next 6 weeks using organic social media and paid

advertising" is a time-bound goal that provides a concrete deadline.

Putting It All Together

By defining your social media goals using the SMART framework, you can create a clear roadmap for success. Here's an example of how to set a SMART social media goal:

Goal: "Grow Instagram followers by 25% (from 2,000 to 2,500) over the next 2 months by posting daily content, engaging with followers, and running a targeted ad campaign."

This goal is **Specific** (increase followers), **Measurable** (25% increase), **Achievable** (with daily posts and ads), **Relevant** (growing followers aligns with overall brand awareness objectives), and **Time-bound** (2 months).

By following the SMART criteria, you can ensure that your social media activities are purposeful and measurable, ultimately helping you achieve meaningful business results. Each post, interaction, and campaign should be guided by your goals, making every effort count toward your business growth and success.

Choosing the Right Social Media Platforms

Not all social media platforms are created equal. Each platform caters to different types of audiences and offers unique features that can be leveraged to achieve specific business goals. Choosing the right platforms is essential for reaching your target audience effectively and maximizing your return on investment. Selecting the wrong platform, or spreading your efforts too thin across many platforms, can result in ineffective campaigns. Let's dive into the key platforms, explore their features, and discuss how to select the best ones for your business.

Overview of Key Platforms

Facebook

Audience: With over 2.9 billion monthly active users, Facebook is ideal for reaching a broad demographic, especially adults aged 25-54. It's also popular with users from various income levels, locations, and interests, making it one of the most versatile platforms.

Best for: Building a community, customer engagement, targeted advertising, and sharing long-form content like blog posts and videos.

Pros:

- Extensive ad targeting options based on interests, demographics, behaviors, and more.

- A wide user base allows businesses to reach a large audience.

- A variety of content formats such as status updates, photos, videos, events, and live streaming.

Cons:

- Organic reach has significantly declined, meaning businesses need to invest in paid ads to effectively reach their audience.

Instagram

Audience: Primarily popular among younger users aged 18-34, with a focus on visual content like images, videos, and stories. It's a visually-driven platform ideal for lifestyle, fashion, and creative businesses.

Best for: Branding, showcasing products, influencer marketing, and engaging younger, trend-driven audiences.

Pros:

- High engagement rates, particularly with visually appealing content.
- Features like Instagram Reels and Stories provide additional opportunities for brand visibility.
- Excellent for visual storytelling, allowing businesses to create authentic and creative content.

Cons:

- Limited link-sharing options (links can only be shared in bio or through Instagram Stories if you have a business account).
- Requires consistent posting and creative content creation to maintain engagement.

LinkedIn

Audience: A professional network, with users typically aged 25-49, which makes it ideal for B2B marketing, job seekers, and industry professionals. The platform is more formal and career-oriented.

Best for: B2B marketing, building thought leadership, networking, and recruitment.

Pros:

- Strong organic reach for business-related content.
- Excellent for building authority and credibility in your industry through thought leadership posts and articles.
- Great for professional networking and finding potential business partners, employees, or clients.

Cons:

- Less effective for businesses targeting consumers directly (B2C).
- Visual content may not be as impactful compared to other platforms like Instagram or TikTok.

Twitter

Audience: Known for real-time updates, Twitter is popular with users who are interested in news, trends, and fast-paced conversations. It's a platform for instant engagement and discussion.

Best for: Customer support, real-time brand interaction, engaging with trending topics, and building brand voice.

Pros:

- Fast-paced engagement, ideal for joining ongoing conversations or reacting to breaking news.
- Excellent for customer service, addressing concerns, and building brand loyalty through quick replies.
- Great for real-time marketing and keeping your audience updated.

Cons:

- Limited character count requires concise, sharp messaging.
- Content lifespan is short, meaning your messages often get buried quickly, which requires constant activity.

TikTok

Audience: Dominated by Gen Z and younger Millennials, TikTok is focused on short-form video content that's often humorous, creative, and visually dynamic. This platform thrives on viral content and creativity.

Best for: Viral marketing, brand awareness, and engaging with a younger demographic who values entertainment and trends.

Pros:

- High potential for viral content due to the platform's algorithm and the ability to trend quickly.

- Strong user engagement, particularly with entertaining or relatable videos.

- Creative video editing tools and effects allow for a variety of content styles.

Cons:

- Requires regular video content creation, which can be time-consuming.

- The content demands creativity and consistency to capture attention and stand out from the noise.

Pinterest

Audience: Predominantly female users, Pinterest is popular with individuals seeking inspiration, particularly in categories like DIY, fashion, home decor, and recipes.

Best for: Driving traffic to websites, particularly for e-commerce brands, bloggers, and creators looking to share inspiration or ideas.

Pros:

- Strong visual search capabilities, enabling users to discover products or ideas based on images.

- Excellent for evergreen content, as pins often continue to drive traffic long after they are posted.

- Great for visual storytelling and showcasing creative products or services.

Cons:

- Limited interaction with followers compared to other platforms, making it more of a passive engagement tool.

- Audience is more niche, so it may not be effective for all types of businesses.

How to Select the Best Platforms for Your Business

Choosing the right social media platforms involves understanding your audience, content, resources, and goals.

Here are some key considerations to help you make the right choice:

1. Understand Your Target Audience

To effectively reach your audience, you need to know where they spend their time online. Analyze your existing customer base and consider factors such as age, gender, location, interests, and behaviors. Social media analytics tools (like Google Analytics or native platform insights) can provide valuable data to help identify which platforms drive the most traffic to your website.

> **Example**: If your target audience is primarily teenagers and young adults, TikTok or Instagram may be the best platforms for you. If you're targeting professionals or business clients, LinkedIn could be more effective.

2. Define Your Content Style

Consider the type of content your brand creates. Social media platforms cater to different content formats, so it's crucial to align your content style with the platform's strengths.

- **Example**: If your brand relies on visuals, such as fashion, food, or design, Instagram and Pinterest are excellent choices. If you share more industry-related insights, LinkedIn might be the best place for thought leadership content.

3. Consider Your Resources

Managing multiple platforms can be time-consuming and resource-intensive. Start with one or two platforms where your audience is most active and focus on growing those channels before expanding. If you're a small business with limited resources, it's better to excel on one platform rather than spread yourself too thin.

- **Example:** If you have limited time, you might start with Instagram to showcase products visually and grow your presence, then expand to other platforms like Facebook or Twitter once you have more resources.

4. Evaluate Platform Features

Each platform has unique features that can enhance your marketing strategy. For example, Instagram's Stories feature can help boost engagement, while LinkedIn Articles can position you as an industry expert. Evaluate the features of each platform to determine which align best with your business objectives.

> **Example:** If you want to run targeted ad campaigns, Facebook offers extensive ad targeting options. If you're focused on influencer marketing, Instagram and TikTok are platforms where you can find the most effective influencers for your brand.

By understanding the unique characteristics of each platform, you can make an informed decision on where to focus your social media marketing efforts. Choose platforms that align with your business goals, resonate with your audience, and offer features that support your content and engagement strategies.

Creating a Social Media Strategy

Having a presence on social media is great, but without a strategy, you're simply shooting in the dark. A well-defined social media strategy is essential for maximizing your efforts and achieving your business goals.

The Importance of a Social Media Strategy:

A strategy helps you stay consistent, allocate resources effectively, and measure your success. It's the blueprint for everything you do on social media, guiding your content creation, engagement tactics, and performance analysis. A solid strategy will allow you to:

- Stay focused on your business objectives.

- Build a recognizable and cohesive brand presence.

- Make data-driven decisions to continuously improve your social media efforts.

Steps to Build a Solid Strategy:

Audience Analysis:

- Understanding your target audience is the foundation of any successful social media strategy. Start by creating detailed buyer personas that capture the demographics (age, gender, location), interests, challenges, and online behavior of your ideal customers.

- Use tools like **Facebook Insights**, **Instagram Analytics**, and **LinkedIn Demographics** to gather insights about your current followers. These platforms provide invaluable data on who's engaging with your content, which can help you fine-tune your content and engagement tactics.

- Conduct surveys or interviews to dig deeper into your audience's preferences. The more you know about their needs, the better you can create content that resonates with them.

Define Your Content Pillars:

- Content pillars are overarching themes that guide the type of content you will consistently post. These pillars should align with your brand's voice, values, and business objectives. For example, if you're in the wellness industry, your content pillars might be **Health Tips**, **Motivational Content**, and **Client Success Stories**.

- These pillars help you stay focused and consistent in your messaging, ensuring that everything you post serves a clear purpose and appeals to your audience's needs and desires.

- Content pillars also make it easier to brainstorm ideas and create a balanced mix of posts. Whether you're posting educational, entertaining, or promotional content, make sure it supports one of your key pillars.

Develop a Content Calendar:

- A content calendar is essential for planning and scheduling posts ahead of time. It ensures that you're consistently posting without scrambling for content ideas on the fly.

- Your calendar should include a diverse mix of content types, such as **promotional posts**, **educational content**, **user-generated content**, and **engagement-focused posts**. This variety keeps your feed dynamic and helps you cater to different audience preferences.

- Include important dates (holidays, events, product launches) and trends that can inform your content. Use scheduling tools like **Buffer**, **Hootsuite**, or **Later** to plan and automate your posts across multiple platforms.

Engagement Tactics:

- Engagement is one of the most important aspects of social media. It's not enough to just post content; you need to actively build relationships with your audience.

- Respond to comments, messages, and mentions promptly to foster a sense of community. Host live Q&A sessions, run polls, and ask open-ended questions to encourage interaction.

- Utilize interactive features on platforms like **Instagram Stories' question stickers, Facebook polls**, or **Twitter chats** to make your posts more engaging.

- Don't just wait for your audience to come to you— actively participate in industry conversations. Join relevant hashtags, comment on popular posts, and share valuable insights to increase visibility and show your brand's expertise.

Competitor Analysis:

- Understanding what your competitors are doing on social media can give you a competitive edge. Study their content strategies to identify what's working and where there's room for improvement.

- Tools like **BuzzSumo, Sprout Social**, and **Social Blade** can help you track your competitors' performance and uncover the type of content that resonates with their followers. Pay attention to their posting frequency, the hashtags they use, and the engagement they're generating.

- While you don't want to copy competitors, looking at their strengths and weaknesses can help you discover opportunities to differentiate your brand and fill gaps in the market.

Set Key Performance Indicators (KPIs):

- Once your strategy is in place, you need to determine how you will measure success. KPIs help you assess the effectiveness of your social media efforts and guide your future actions.

- Common KPIs include **follower growth, engagement rates, click-through rates, conversion rates,** and **brand mentions**. Your KPIs should align with your business goals and the specific objectives of your social media strategy.

- Use analytics tools like **Google Analytics, Hootsuite,** or **Sprout Social** to track your KPIs across all platforms. This data will provide you with actionable insights into what's working and where improvements can be made.

Recap of the Process:

A successful social media strategy involves a comprehensive approach, starting with understanding your audience and content themes, followed by planning, creating engaging content, analyzing competitors, and regularly measuring success with KPIs. Stay flexible and ready to adjust your strategy as needed based on performance data and market changes. This approach will help you build a strong and sustainable social media presence that aligns with your business objectives.

Conclusion

Getting started with social media may seem overwhelming, but with the right approach, it can be one of the most rewarding marketing channels for your small business. By defining clear goals, choosing the right platforms, and developing a solid strategy, you can build a strong social media presence that drives brand awareness, customer engagement, and sales.

In the next chapter, we will dive deeper into content creation and explore how to craft compelling posts that resonate with your audience and drive engagement. Stay tuned for tips, tricks, and best practices to make your social media content shine!

Chapter 2: Optimizing Your Social Media Profiles

Your social media profiles are the face of your brand online. They often serve as the first point of contact for potential customers, so it's essential to make a strong first impression. An optimized social media profile can help you build credibility, attract followers, and improve your visibility in search results. In this chapter, we'll cover the key steps to setting up your social media profiles for success, maintaining brand consistency across platforms, and leveraging platform-specific features to maximize engagement.

Setting Up Your Profiles for Success

The foundation of a strong social media presence starts with a well-optimized profile. Your social media profiles are often the first interaction potential customers have with your brand, so it's crucial to ensure they reflect your business professionally and attractively. Here's how to ensure your social media profiles are set up to attract and engage your target audience.

Profile and Cover Photo Best Practices

Choose High-Quality Images:

Profile Picture: Your profile picture is often the first thing users see when they land on your page, so it should be clear, high-resolution, and instantly recognizable. For most businesses, using your **logo** as the profile picture is a good choice, as it reinforces brand recognition and professionalism.

> **Pro Tip:** If you're a personal brand or influencer, a clear, well-lit headshot might be more appropriate.

Cover Photo: Your cover photo is a larger visual space and can be used to showcase key aspects of your business. Use it as an opportunity to highlight your latest promotion, product, or event. It should be visually appealing and in line with your branding.

> **Pro Tip:** Consider changing your cover photo regularly to highlight seasonal promotions, new services, or events. This keeps your profile fresh and engaging.

Maintain Consistency Across Platforms:

- **Consistency:** Consistency in your profile image and cover photo across all social media channels is crucial. It helps users easily recognize your brand across different platforms, which builds trust and brand recall.

Pro Tip: Ensure your branding remains cohesive, using similar colors, fonts, and images across all platforms.

Platform-Specific Optimization: Each social media platform has its own image size requirements, and ensuring your photos are properly sized is essential for visual clarity and professionalism. Here are some general size recommendations:

- **Facebook profile picture:** 170 x 170 pixels
- **Instagram profile picture:** 110 x 110 pixels
- **LinkedIn profile picture:** 400 x 400 pixels
- **Twitter profile picture:** 400 x 400 pixels
- **Cover photo sizes:** Facebook: 820 x 312 pixels; Twitter: 1500 x 500 pixels; LinkedIn: 1584 x 396 pixels

Pro Tip: Always preview your profile photos on each platform to ensure they appear correctly, without being cropped awkwardly.

Crafting a Compelling Bio and Using Keywords Effectively

Your bio is a short but powerful piece of content that can influence whether someone follows you or not. A compelling bio should clearly communicate who you are, what you do, and the value you provide. It's your digital elevator pitch.

Make It Clear and Concise:

Your bio should be **direct** and to the point. Focus on what makes your business unique, and clearly explain why users should follow you.

Pro Tip: Avoid jargon and long-winded explanations. A concise bio makes it easier for visitors to immediately understand your brand's value.

Include a Call-to-Action (CTA): Adding a CTA in your bio encourages visitors to take the next step. Whether it's visiting your website, signing up for a newsletter, or contacting you for more information, having a CTA prompts action.

Example: "Visit our website for exclusive deals!" or "DM us to learn more about our services!"

Use Keywords Strategically:

Keywords help users find your profile through social media searches. Think about the terms your target audience might use to find businesses like yours and include them naturally in your bio.

- **Example:** If you're a digital marketing agency, include keywords like "social media marketing," "SEO services," or "content creation" in your bio to increase discoverability.

    Pro Tip: Avoid keyword stuffing—incorporate relevant keywords in a way that still feels natural and conversational.

Include Contact Information:

Make It Easy to Connect: Ensure users can easily reach out to you. Include your contact information, such as an email address, phone number, or a link to your website. This makes it easier for potential clients to get in touch.

> **Pro Tip:** On platforms like **Instagram** and **Facebook**, take advantage of the "contact" button features to allow users to reach you directly.

- **Optional Links:** Some social media platforms, like **Instagram** and **Twitter**, allow you to include additional links in your bio. Use this feature to link to important resources, like your blog, product page, or booking system.

How to Optimize Your Profiles for SEO

Optimizing your social media profiles for search engines can increase your visibility, both on the platform and in Google search results. Here are some tips for improving your SEO and driving traffic to your profile.

Use Your Brand Name Consistently:

- **Username/Handle Consistency:** Your username or handle should be the same across all platforms. This makes it easier for users to find you and reinforces brand recognition.

- **Include Your Business Name in Key Areas:** Ensure your business name appears in your profile's **display name** and **bio**. This improves your searchability, both within social platforms and on Google.

> **Pro Tip:** If your business name is commonly searched, incorporating it into your profile boosts your chances of showing up in relevant searches.

Include Relevant Keywords in Your Bio and Posts:

- **Bio Optimization:** Incorporate industry-specific keywords that your target audience might be searching for. For example, if you run a fitness business, you might include keywords like "personal training," "fitness tips," or "workout routines" in your bio.

  > **Pro Tip:** Be sure to include **location-based keywords** as well, especially if you offer services in a specific geographic area.

- **Post Optimization:** Optimize your posts by including relevant hashtags, keywords, and location tags. This increases your visibility in hashtag searches and helps your posts get discovered by a broader audience.

Optimize Links in Your Bio:

- **Link to Valuable Resources:** Use the link in your bio to drive traffic to specific landing pages, special promotions, or your latest blog post. This is an important part of conversion and tracking success.

- **Tools for Multiple Links:** Platforms like **Linktree** or **Beacons** can help you include multiple links in one place, which is especially useful for Instagram. These tools allow you to direct traffic to various destinations without cluttering your bio with multiple URLs.

  > **Pro Tip:** Update the link in your bio regularly to reflect current promotions, new products, or seasonal campaigns.

Final Thoughts

A well-optimized social media profile is essential for attracting and retaining followers. By choosing high-quality images, crafting a compelling bio, using keywords effectively, and optimizing your profiles for SEO, you can significantly improve your visibility and engagement on social media. Keep your branding consistent across platforms, and ensure your contact information is easy to find. With these strategies in place, you'll be able to attract the right audience and drive meaningful interactions on your social media pages.

Branding Your Social Media

Consistency is the cornerstone of successful branding on social media. A cohesive and recognizable brand identity can make your business stand out, build trust with your audience, and enhance your marketing efforts. Ensuring a unified look and feel across all your social platforms strengthens brand recognition and makes your business more memorable. Below are essential tips for branding your social media presence.

Ensuring Brand Consistency Across Platforms

Use a Consistent Color Scheme:

Color Palette: A well-chosen color scheme is a powerful tool in branding. It helps create a visual connection between your content and your brand. Consistently using a set of brand colors across all your social media channels ensures that your content is immediately recognizable.

> **Pro Tip:** Choose colors that reflect your brand personality and values. For example, blue often represents trust and professionalism, while green can symbolize sustainability and health.

- **Tools for Consistency:** Platforms like **Canva** allow you to save your brand colors in your account settings. This makes it easy to access and apply your brand's color palette when creating social media graphics. Consistency is key, and color tools streamline the process.

> **Pro Tip:** Use color psychology to enhance your brand's emotional appeal. For example, red can evoke excitement or urgency, while soft pastels may create a calming effect.

Maintain a Consistent Tone of Voice:

Voice Consistency: Your brand's tone of voice should reflect the essence of your company and its values. Whether your tone is professional, friendly, humorous, or authoritative, it's essential to maintain that same tone across all platforms.

> **Pro Tip:** Align your tone with your audience's expectations. For example, a tech company might adopt a more authoritative tone, while a fashion brand might use a fun and conversational voice.

- **Captions and Messages:** Use the same tone in your social media captions, comments, direct messages, and responses. Whether you're sharing educational content or responding to customer inquiries, consistency in communication helps build a stronger emotional connection with your audience.

- **Style Guide:** A **brand style guide** is a useful tool for ensuring tone consistency. Include clear instructions for your tone of voice, language preferences, the use of emojis, and overall messaging style. This guide can be shared with your social media team to ensure alignment across all communication channels.

Use Branded Hashtags:

- **Hashtag Strategy:** Branded hashtags are a great way to create a sense of community and increase the reach of your content. A unique hashtag makes it easier for users to find and engage with your brand's posts, and it also helps track campaign success.

  > **Example:** Nike's #JustDoIt is one of the most recognizable branded hashtags in the world, allowing users to share content aligned with Nike's values and ethos.

- **User-Generated Content:** Encourage your followers to use your branded hashtag when posting about your products or services. This not only increases engagement but also gives you the chance to feature user-generated content on your profile.

  > **Pro Tip:** Hold contests or giveaways where users must use your branded hashtag to participate. This increases visibility and encourages followers to share content on your behalf.

Using Brand Guidelines to Maintain a Cohesive Online Presence

Create a Social Media Style Guide:

Consistency in Design and Messaging: A comprehensive **social media style guide** ensures that everyone on your team understands how to represent your brand across different platforms. It should include key elements like:

Logo Usage: Provide clear rules about how your logo should be used, including any restrictions on resizing, colors, or background placement.

Color Codes: List the exact color codes (RGB, Hex, or Pantone) to ensure consistency in all designs.

Fonts and Typography: Include the fonts you use for both digital and print materials. Whether you use custom fonts or standard ones like Arial or Helvetica, consistent typography reinforces brand identity.

Messaging and Tone: As mentioned earlier, clarify your brand's tone and style of communication, ensuring everyone is on the same page when creating content.

Image Styles: Define the types of images you want to use—whether stock photos, original images, or illustrations—and what style or theme they should convey (e.g., lifestyle, minimalistic, vibrant).

> **Pro Tip:** Share your social media style guide with anyone who works on your social media accounts, including freelancers or external agencies. This ensures that all content created aligns with your brand's vision.

Use Templates for Social Media Graphics:

Design Consistency: Templates are an excellent way to maintain a uniform look and feel for all your social media posts, stories, and ads. Using templates ensures that your content adheres to your brand's color scheme, typography, and overall design style.

> **Pro Tip:** Create different templates for various types of content, such as promotional posts, announcements, quotes, or event invitations. This allows you to quickly create consistent, on-brand content without starting from scratch each time.

Time-Saving: Templates save time and effort. Platforms like **Canva**, **Adobe Spark**, and other design tools offer customizable templates tailored to various social media platforms, making it easy to create high-quality content quickly.

> **Pro Tip:** Consider building templates for each platform's specific requirements (e.g., Instagram stories, Facebook posts, Pinterest pins) to optimize the design for each medium. This ensures that content looks polished and professional no matter where it's shared.

Final Thoughts

Brand consistency on social media is essential for building a strong, recognizable identity. By using a consistent color scheme, maintaining a cohesive tone of voice, and implementing branded hashtags, you reinforce your brand's image and make it more memorable. Establishing a **social media style guide** and using templates for design will help streamline the process and ensure consistency across your content. As you continue to create and share content, your brand's consistent presence will build trust, engagement, and loyalty with your audience.

Utilizing Social Media Features

Each social media platform offers a unique set of features that can elevate your content strategy, engage your audience, and increase visibility. Knowing how to leverage these features can give your social media presence a competitive edge, helping you stand out and drive more traffic to your business.

How to Make the Most of Social Media Features

Instagram Stories and Highlights:

- **Behind-the-Scenes Content:** Instagram Stories are perfect for sharing real-time content, giving your followers an inside look at your business. You can show behind-the-scenes footage, share sneak peeks of upcoming products, or give followers a glimpse into the day-to-day operations of your business.

  Pro Tip: Use Stories to promote limited-time offers or flash sales, as the temporary nature of Stories creates urgency and encourages quick action.

- **Engagement Tools:** Engage your audience directly by using interactive features such as polls, quizzes, sliders, and question stickers. These tools can increase audience interaction and provide valuable insights into what your followers are interested in.

  Pro Tip: Use the "Questions" feature to ask for feedback, opinions, or suggestions, which can help you better understand your audience's needs and preferences.

- **Instagram Highlights:** Organize your most engaging Stories into Highlights to keep them visible beyond their

24-hour lifespan. You can create Highlight collections for specific topics such as products, testimonials, behind-the-scenes content, or events.

> **Pro Tip:** Regularly update your Highlights with fresh content to keep it relevant and interesting for new followers.

- **Link Sticker Feature:** Instagram's Link Sticker allows you to add clickable links to your Stories, making it easier for users to visit your website, shop, or explore other pages.

> **Pro Tip:** Use this feature to drive traffic to specific landing pages, new blog posts, or product pages, and make sure to add a call-to-action (CTA) that encourages users to click the link.

LinkedIn Articles and Posts:

- **Long-Form Content with LinkedIn Articles:** LinkedIn provides an excellent opportunity to establish your authority in your industry through long-form content. Use LinkedIn Articles to dive deeper into relevant topics, showcase your expertise, and share insights that add value to your audience.

> **Pro Tip:** Write well-researched articles that provide actionable advice, industry trends, or case studies. LinkedIn's professional audience will appreciate this high-quality content.

- **Regular Posts for Engagement:** Alongside Articles, use LinkedIn's regular post feature to share updates, company news, and thought-provoking insights. Short posts are a great way to keep your network engaged without overwhelming them with lengthy articles.

> **Pro Tip:** Use a mix of post types—such as polls, shareable images, and videos—to keep your audience engaged and encourage comments.

- **Showcase Products and Services:** LinkedIn's company page features allow you to highlight specific products or services. Use these sections to detail your offerings, post updates, and respond to inquiries. This can help you build a professional presence and attract potential clients or customers.

> **Pro Tip:** Encourage employees to engage with your posts and share your content to increase reach and credibility.

Facebook Groups:

- **Create or Join Relevant Groups:** Facebook Groups are an excellent way to build a community around your brand. Whether you create your own group or join industry-specific groups, this feature allows you to engage with like-minded individuals, share knowledge, and build relationships.

> **Pro Tip:** When creating a group, focus on adding value by providing exclusive content, hosting live discussions, or offering expert advice. This will help position your brand as a valuable resource within the group.

- **Engage with Group Members:** Actively participate in discussions, answer questions, and share relevant resources to build trust and establish authority in your field.

> **Pro Tip:** Use the group to ask for feedback, conduct surveys, or gather insights that will inform your business decisions or product development.

- **Market Research and Customer Support:** Facebook Groups can also serve as a valuable tool for market research, allowing you to understand your audience's preferences and pain points. Additionally, they can act as a space for customer support, where members can help each other and share their experiences with your products or services.

> **Pro Tip:** Use the group as a forum to offer exclusive customer support or troubleshoot common issues, positioning your brand as responsive and customer-centric.

The Power of Hashtags, Geotags, and Tagging Other Accounts

Hashtags:

- **Boost Reach with Hashtags:** Hashtags help increase the visibility of your content on social media by categorizing it for users interested in specific topics. Use a strategic mix of popular, niche, and branded hashtags to expand the reach of your posts.

> **Pro Tip:** Combine broad hashtags (e.g., #MarketingTips) with more specific or niche hashtags (e.g., #SocialMediaStrategy) to target both a larger audience and a more engaged, specific group.

- **Research Trending Hashtags:** Stay on top of industry trends by using hashtag research tools such as **Hashtagify, All Hashtag,** or **RiteTag**. These tools can help you discover trending hashtags that align with your brand and content.

  > **Pro Tip:** Participate in trending conversations by using relevant hashtags, increasing your chances of reaching new users who are actively following those topics.

Geotags:

Localize Your Content with Geotags: Adding location tags (geotags) to your social media posts can help you reach local audiences and attract potential customers in your area. This is especially beneficial for businesses with a physical presence, such as restaurants, retail stores, or service providers.

> **Pro Tip:** If you're hosting an event or offering a special promotion, geotagging your content can drive foot traffic and help potential customers find your location easily.

Increase Local Visibility: Geotags on Instagram and Facebook allow users to search for content related to specific locations. For example, if someone is searching for cafes in their city, they can discover your posts by filtering for content tagged with your location.

> **Pro Tip:** Encourage customers to geotag their own photos when they visit your location, further increasing your brand's local visibility.

Tagging Other Accounts:

Collaborate and Expand Reach: Tagging relevant accounts—such as influencers, partners, or customers—in your posts can increase engagement and broaden your reach. When you tag someone, it notifies them, often leading to more interactions with your content.

> **Pro Tip:** Tag influencers or other brands in your industry when you share content that involves them, whether it's a product collaboration, event participation, or shared values.

Building Partnerships through Tagging: Tagging partners, sponsors, or collaborators in your posts helps create visibility for both parties and strengthens relationships within your industry.

> **Pro Tip:** Use tagging as part of your partnership and collaboration strategies. For example, tag a brand you're working with to amplify your message and reach a wider audience.

Final Thoughts

Maximizing social media features is essential for creating engaging, shareable content that increases visibility and drives business growth. Features like **Instagram Stories**, **LinkedIn Articles**, **Facebook Groups**, and the strategic use of **hashtags**, **geotags**, and **tagging** other accounts allow you to connect with your audience, enhance your brand's reach, and build a loyal community. By incorporating these features into your social media strategy, you can stay ahead of the competition and ensure your business stands out across platforms.

Conclusion

Optimizing your social media profiles is a crucial step toward establishing a strong online presence. By setting up your profiles correctly, maintaining brand consistency, and utilizing platform-specific features, you can effectively engage with your audience and achieve your business goals.

In the next chapter, we will explore content creation in detail, focusing on how to develop engaging posts, use visuals effectively, and create a content calendar that aligns with your social media strategy. Get ready to dive into the art of social media storytelling!

Chapter 3: Creating Engaging Content

Creating engaging content is the cornerstone of any successful social media strategy. Whether you're aiming to boost brand awareness, increase engagement, or drive conversions, the content you share plays a critical role in achieving these goals. This chapter will guide you through understanding your audience, developing content that resonates, utilizing the right tools, and crafting compelling captions that captivate your followers.

Understanding Your Audience

Before diving into content creation, it's crucial to understand who you're speaking to. Knowing your audience enables you to craft messages, choose visuals, and develop a tone that resonates with their preferences, leading to better engagement, stronger relationships, and more impactful results. A deep understanding of your audience forms the foundation for any successful content strategy.

Building Detailed Audience Personas

1. What Are Audience Personas?

Definition: Audience personas are semi-fictional representations of your ideal customers. These personas are created based on comprehensive market research and real data gathered from your existing customer base. They help you understand your audience's demographics, motivations, challenges, and behaviors.

Purpose: Personas serve as a roadmap for content creation. By knowing who your audience is, you can tailor your content to meet their needs, address their pain points, and speak in a voice they relate to. This leads to more relevant and engaging content that drives conversions and builds long-term relationships.

> **Pro Tip:** While personas are based on real data, they should also incorporate assumptions or "best guesses" where data may be limited. As you gather more insights, you can refine and adjust these personas over time.

2. Steps to Build Audience Personas:

Gather Data: The first step in creating personas is gathering demographic and behavioral data from your audience. Analytics tools like **Google Analytics, Facebook Insights,** and **Instagram Analytics** can provide you with valuable information about your audience's age, gender, location, interests, and behavior patterns. These tools allow you to look at data such as what pages your audience visits, how long they stay, and what content they interact with.

Pro Tip: Don't just focus on the numbers—dig deeper into qualitative data such as sentiment analysis (how your audience feels about certain topics) and specific keywords or phrases they use when interacting with your content.

Conduct Surveys and Interviews: To gain a more nuanced understanding, reach out directly to your current customers through surveys, interviews, or focus groups. Ask about their challenges, goals, and what they value most. This firsthand feedback helps you uncover emotional triggers, customer motivations, and specific pain points that numbers alone might not reveal.

Pro Tip: Incentivize survey participation with discounts or exclusive content to encourage more responses.

Define Key Characteristics: With the data you've gathered, start creating a profile for your ideal audience member. Key characteristics to include are:

- **Demographics:** Age, gender, location, income, occupation, education level

- **Psychographics:** Interests, values, personality traits, lifestyle

- **Goals:** What are they trying to achieve? What problems are they solving?

- **Challenges:** What obstacles do they face in reaching their goals? What are their pain points?

- **Preferred Platforms and Content Types:** Where do they spend their time online? Do they prefer video, articles, or infographics? What social media platforms do they frequent?

Example Persona:

- **Name:** Sarah, the Eco-Conscious Shopper

- **Age:** 28

- **Occupation:** Marketing Professional

- **Interests:** Sustainable living, DIY projects, plant-based diets, minimalism

- **Social Media Platforms:** Instagram, Pinterest

- **Goals:** Sarah is passionate about reducing her environmental footprint. She is actively seeking eco-friendly product recommendations and is interested in sustainable brands that align with her values.

- **Challenges:** Sarah struggles to find trustworthy brands that are truly eco-conscious and not just greenwashing.

- **Content Preferences:** Sarah loves well-designed, informative content that is focused on sustainability, DIY tips, and natural living. She engages with brands that provide practical advice, transparency, and authenticity.

> **Pro Tip:** The more specific and detailed your persona, the easier it is to tailor your content strategy and messaging to meet their needs.

The Role of Social Listening and Audience Research

What Is Social Listening?

Definition: Social listening is the process of monitoring social media platforms and online channels for mentions of your brand, competitors, industry topics, and general trends. It involves actively listening to what people are saying about your brand and how they're interacting with your content. This practice allows you to gather actionable insights and respond promptly to customer sentiment.

Tools: There are various tools available for effective social listening, including **Sprout Social, Brandwatch, Mention, and Hootsuite Insights**. These platforms help track mentions, keywords, hashtags, and sentiment across social channels.

> **Pro Tip:** Set up alerts for specific keywords related to your brand, product, or industry. This enables you to stay ahead of trends and spot potential PR opportunities or challenges.

Benefits of Social Listening:

Discover Content Ideas: By listening to your audience's conversations, you can identify common pain points, frequently asked questions, and trending topics. These insights allow you to create content that speaks directly to your audience's current concerns and interests.

> **Pro Tip:** Use social listening to track real-time conversations around events, holidays, or industry-specific trends. This can help you produce timely and relevant content, positioning your brand as an authoritative voice in your field.

Improve Customer Service: Social listening enables you to monitor customer feedback and respond in real time.

Engaging with your audience when they mention your brand, ask questions, or share feedback demonstrates that you value their input. It strengthens customer loyalty and enhances your brand's reputation.

> **Pro Tip:** Set up automatic notifications to alert you when people mention your brand so you can address concerns immediately. A timely response can prevent issues from escalating and show customers that you care.

Refine Your Strategy: By consistently analyzing what content resonates with your audience and what topics are gaining traction, you can refine your content strategy and adjust your approach. Social listening also allows you to monitor competitor activity, providing insights into what is working for them and where there may be opportunities to differentiate your brand.

> **Pro Tip:** Track key performance indicators (KPIs) like engagement rates, sentiment, and share of voice to assess the effectiveness of your social media campaigns and identify areas for improvement.

> **Pro Tip:** Social listening isn't just about monitoring brand mentions—it's also about understanding your audience's broader conversations, enabling you to stay relevant and responsive.

Conclusion

Understanding your audience is the cornerstone of successful content marketing. By building detailed audience personas and employing social listening strategies, you can craft more targeted content that resonates with your ideal customers. This approach not only drives better engagement but also fosters stronger, more lasting relationships with your audience. Whether you're gathering data through analytics or engaging in conversations through social listening, the key is to remain focused on your audience's needs, challenges, and desires to ensure your content strategy hits the mark.

Types of Content That Work

A successful social media content strategy involves using a variety of content types to keep your audience engaged and encourage interaction. Each content format serves a different purpose, from driving sales to building brand loyalty. Below, we'll explore the key content types that work best on social media and why they should be part of your strategy.

The Content Mix: Promotional, Educational, Inspirational, and Entertaining

Promotional Content:

Purpose: The primary goal of promotional content is to drive sales, generate leads, and promote products or services. It is direct and focuses on converting your audience into customers.

Examples:

- **Product launches:** Announce new products or services to build excitement.
- **Flash sales:** Limited-time offers to create urgency.
- **Discount codes:** Provide exclusive deals to incentivize purchases.

> **Tip:** Always use a **compelling Call to Action (CTA)** that directs users to take immediate action, such as

making a purchase, signing up for your newsletter, or visiting your website. Phrases like "Shop now," "Limited time offer," or "Get your discount today" create urgency and drive conversions.

Example CTA: "Hurry, these deals won't last long! Use code 'SALE20' for 20% off your first order!"

Educational Content:

Purpose: Educational content provides value to your audience by sharing industry knowledge, tips, and actionable insights. It helps establish your brand as an authority and builds trust with your audience.

Examples:

- **How-to guides:** Step-by-step instructions on how to use your product or solve a common problem.
- **Tutorials:** Walkthroughs that teach your audience something new.
- **Infographics:** Visual summaries of complex topics that are easy to digest.
- **Informative blog posts:** Detailed articles that dive into topics your audience cares about.

Tip: Break down complex topics into simple, actionable steps to make them digestible and easy to follow. Visual aids, such as images, charts, and diagrams, help enhance understanding.

Example: "Here's how you can boost your website's SEO in 5 easy steps. Check out our full guide to get started!"

Inspirational Content:

Purpose: Inspirational content motivates and uplifts your audience. It can strengthen emotional connections with your brand and encourage positive feelings about your products or services.

Examples:

- **Quotes:** Positive or motivational quotes that resonate with your audience.
- **Testimonials:** Stories from satisfied customers or clients that highlight your product's effectiveness.
- **Behind-the-scenes stories:** Insights into your brand's values, culture, or development process.
- **Case studies:** Success stories of customers achieving significant results with your product.

> **Tip:** Use **storytelling** to create a narrative that emotionally connects with your audience. Sharing real stories of transformation or success builds authenticity and trust.

Example: "See how our product helped Sarah reduce her stress levels and improve her productivity in just one month!"

Entertaining Content:

Purpose: Entertaining content is designed to engage your audience by making them laugh, sparking curiosity, or providing a fun escape. It is typically light-hearted and shareable.

Examples:

- **Memes:** Humorous images or videos that tap into current trends or relatable moments.
- **Viral challenges:** Participating in trending challenges can increase visibility and engagement.
- **GIFs:** Fun, quick visuals that bring humor or visual context to a message.
- **Light-hearted videos:** Videos that entertain, such as pranks or bloopers, that make your audience smile.

> **Tip:** Leverage **trends** and **pop culture references** to make your content more relatable and timely. Ensure your brand voice matches the tone of the content to maintain authenticity.

Example: "Join us in this viral challenge and show us your skills! Tag us to get featured."

Examples of High-Performing Content (Infographics, Videos, User-Generated Content)

Infographics:

Why They Work: Infographics are visually appealing, concise, and effective at conveying complex information in an easy-to-understand format. Because they are visually engaging and informative, infographics tend to get shared more often, helping you reach a broader audience.

> **Tip:** Use tools like **Canva** or **Piktochart** to create infographics that incorporate key statistics, actionable tips, and important industry data. The use

of vibrant colors, bold typography, and icons can make the information easier to digest.

Example: "Check out our latest infographic on the top 5 SEO trends of 2024!"

Videos:

Why They Work: Videos are one of the most engaging types of content because they combine audio, visuals, and movement to capture attention quickly. They are also more likely to be shared than text or image posts. Videos work well for product demonstrations, tutorials, behind-the-scenes content, or customer testimonials.

> **Tip:** Keep videos **short and impactful**. On platforms like Instagram or Twitter, videos should ideally be under 2 minutes to maintain audience attention. For platforms like YouTube or Facebook, you can experiment with longer-form videos (up to 10 minutes or more). Always prioritize quality content that educates, entertains, or inspires.

Example: "Watch this quick tutorial on how to use our new app feature and start simplifying your workflow today!"

User-Generated Content (UGC):

Why They Work: UGC is content created by your audience, often featuring your product or brand. It builds authenticity and trust because it shows real customers using and enjoying your product. UGC also fosters a sense of community and encourages brand loyalty.

> **Tip:** Encourage your followers to share their experiences with your product and tag your brand in

their posts. You can also run contests or giveaways to incentivize UGC. Reposting UGC on your social media profile not only builds community engagement but also serves as social proof for your brand.

Example: "We love seeing how you use our products! Tag us in your photos for a chance to be featured on our page."

Conclusion

Incorporating a mix of **promotional, educational, inspirational, and entertaining content** into your social media strategy ensures that you cater to a wide range of audience needs and preferences. High-performing content types like **infographics, videos, and user-generated content** can help boost engagement, increase shares, and build a stronger connection with your audience. By maintaining a varied and consistent content strategy, you'll keep your followers engaged, encourage action, and ultimately strengthen your brand's presence and reputation across platforms.

Content Creation Tools and Tips

Creating high-quality content doesn't require an extensive budget or hours of effort. With the right tools and techniques, you can streamline your content creation process while producing professional and engaging content. Below are some recommended tools and tips for graphic design, video editing, and scheduling, as well as advice for improving the quality of your visuals and videos.

Recommended Tools for Graphic Design, Video Editing, and Scheduling

Graphic Design Tools:

Canva:

Why It Works: Canva is one of the most accessible tools for creating professional-looking graphics, infographics, and social media posts. With a wide range of templates, fonts, and design elements, you can easily create visually appealing content.

> **Tip:** Use Canva's **Brand Kit** feature to upload your logo, brand colors, and fonts for consistent design across all your graphics.

Example: Create eye-catching Instagram posts or Facebook ads within minutes using Canva's drag-and-drop interface.

Adobe Spark:

Why It Works: Adobe Spark allows you to create branded content like social graphics, short videos, and web pages. It's especially useful for content that needs a cohesive, professional look, as it integrates seamlessly with other Adobe products.

> **Tip:** Use Adobe Spark's **animation tools** to create dynamic, engaging posts that can capture your audience's attention.

Example: Make branded Instagram Stories or Pinterest pins to stand out visually and keep your audience engaged.

Video Editing Tools:

InShot:

Why It Works: InShot is a user-friendly mobile app for editing videos on your phone. It's perfect for quick edits, such as trimming footage, adding filters, and applying background music. This tool is ideal for short-form videos.

> **Tip:** Utilize **speed adjustment features** to create fast-paced, engaging videos that capture attention quickly.

Example: Edit Instagram Reels or TikTok videos with ease, adding music, effects, and smooth transitions.

CapCut:

Why It Works: CapCut is a comprehensive video editing tool perfect for platforms like TikTok and Instagram Reels. It offers transitions, text overlays, special effects, and other advanced features, all within a user-friendly interface.

> **Tip:** Use **special effects** and transitions creatively to make your content stand out from the crowd and gain more visibility on social platforms.

Example: Create viral-style TikTok videos with creative transitions, catchy music, and text overlays to drive engagement.

Social Media Scheduling Tools:

Buffer:

Why It Works: Buffer is a simple and intuitive social media scheduling tool that allows you to schedule posts in advance, track engagement, and analyze the performance of your content across multiple platforms.

Tip: Use **Buffer's analytics** to review engagement data and optimize your future content strategy based on what resonates most with your audience.

Example: Plan and schedule posts for the upcoming week, ensuring a consistent content flow without the need for constant manual updates.

Hootsuite:

Why It Works: Hootsuite is a robust social media management platform that helps you manage all your accounts in one place. It offers scheduling, performance tracking, and even team collaboration features.

Tip: Use **Hootsuite's AutoSchedule** feature to automatically choose the best times for your posts based on audience activity.

Example: Manage content across Facebook, Instagram, Twitter, and LinkedIn, and track performance with detailed insights and metrics.

Tips for Creating High-Quality Visuals and Videos

Use High-Resolution Images:

Why It Works: High-quality, crisp images give your content a professional look and help maintain your brand's reputation. Blurry or pixelated visuals can create a negative impression and distract your audience from your message.

Tip: When sourcing images, always look for **high-resolution photos**. If you can't shoot original images, use stock photo platforms like **Unsplash** or **Shutterstock** to find polished, professional images that align with your content.

Example: For a fashion brand, use high-resolution images of models wearing your clothes to highlight details and textures that will resonate with your audience.

Leverage Natural Light:

Why It Works: Good lighting can drastically improve the quality of your photos and videos. Natural light, especially during the **golden hour** (just after sunrise or before sunset), gives a soft, flattering glow to your content. It's ideal for lifestyle shoots, product photography, and social media posts.

> **Tip:** Always aim to shoot your photos or videos in well-lit areas, ideally near a large window. If shooting outdoors, consider the time of day for the best natural light.

Example: Film a product demo or lifestyle video in the morning or evening when the light is softer, creating a more inviting atmosphere.

Add Text Overlays and Subtitles:

Why It Works: Text overlays can help highlight key messages, emphasize important details, and guide your audience through your content. Subtitles are particularly essential for videos, as many social media users watch videos without sound. Adding subtitles ensures that your content is accessible and comprehensible even on silent mode.

> **Tip:** When creating videos, include **subtitles** or captions using tools like **Kapwing** or **Clips** to ensure your message is clear, even without sound. For social media posts, use **text overlays** to reinforce the main point of the content.

Example: On Instagram Stories, use text overlays to emphasize important offers or messages and add subtitles to your video to increase engagement among viewers who watch without sound.

Conclusion

Creating high-quality content doesn't have to be difficult or time-consuming. By leveraging **graphic design tools** like Canva and Adobe Spark, **video editing tools** like InShot and CapCut, and **scheduling platforms** such as Buffer and Hootsuite, you can streamline your content creation process. To ensure your content resonates with your audience, focus on using **high-resolution images**, leveraging **natural light**, and adding **text overlays and subtitles** to enhance visual appeal and engagement. With these tools and tips, you can elevate your social media content to a professional level while saving time and effort.

Writing Captivating Captions

Captions are a crucial element of your social media posts. They serve to provide context, highlight your brand's personality, and engage your audience in meaningful ways. A well-crafted caption can spark interest, drive engagement, and encourage followers to take specific actions that align with your business goals. Below, we explore how to write captivating captions that will help you connect with your audience and drive more action.

How to Write Engaging Captions That Drive Action

Start with a Hook:

Why It Works: The first line of your caption is the most important because it determines whether someone will keep reading. It should grab attention immediately.

> **Tip:** Use questions, bold statements, or surprising facts that make people curious to read more.

Example: "Did you know that 80% of consumers are more likely to purchase from brands they follow on social media?"

Why It's Effective: This statistic is compelling and makes the reader want to know more, setting the stage for further engagement.

Keep It Conversational:

Why It Works: Social media is a platform for informal communication. Writing captions in a conversational tone makes your brand seem more approachable and relatable.

> **Tip:** Address your audience as though you're speaking to a friend. Use casual language and throw in a few emojis to make the post feel warm and inviting.

Example: "Hey, did you get a chance to check out our new collection yet? 🛍️ Let us know which piece is your favorite! 🙌 "

Why It's Effective: A friendly, informal tone makes people feel like they're part of a conversation, increasing the likelihood of interaction.

Use Hashtags Wisely:

Why It Works: Hashtags increase the visibility of your posts and help new users find your content. They also categorize content, making it easier for people interested in specific topics to discover your brand.

> **Tip:** Use a mix of popular, niche, and branded hashtags. Keep it relevant to your content and your audience.

Example: For a skincare brand, you could use hashtags like #SkincareRoutine, #HealthySkin, and a unique hashtag like #GlowWithUs.

Why It's Effective: This combination broadens your post's reach without overwhelming your followers with too many hashtags.

Using Storytelling to Connect with Your Audience

Share Personal Stories:

Why It Works: People love stories because they humanize your brand and create an emotional connection. By sharing your brand's journey or behind-the-scenes insights, you allow your audience to relate to your values and mission.

> **Tip:** Share anecdotes about your brand's origins, challenges, or success stories that resonate with your audience.

Example: "When we started our bakery, we only had a small oven and a dream. Fast forward to today, and we're so proud to see our little treats making a big impact in the community. 🤍"

Why It's Effective: A personal story adds depth to your brand, helping followers feel more connected to what you do and why you do it.

Incorporate User-Generated Content:

Why It Works: User-generated content (UGC) serves as authentic social proof, showing real customers enjoying or using your products. UGC not only builds trust but also makes other followers feel encouraged to engage with your brand.

> **Tip:** Ask your customers to share their experiences with your products, and feature their stories on your profile.

Example: "We're loving how @user_name styled our latest collection! 😍 Tag us in your photos to get featured. #BrandNameStyle"

Why It's Effective: Featuring real customer stories makes your brand feel more relatable and trustworthy, encouraging further engagement.

The Importance of CTAs (Call to Actions) in Social Posts

What Is a CTA?

Why It Works: A **Call to Action (CTA)** is a prompt that encourages users to take a specific action. Whether you want followers to visit your website, make a purchase, or join a community, a strong CTA can guide them toward that goal.

> **Tip:** A clear and compelling CTA increases the chances of driving conversions and boosting engagement.

Example: "Tap the link in our bio to shop now!" or "Sign up today for 20% off your first order!"

Examples of Effective CTAs:

Why It Works: Effective CTAs are actionable, direct, and create a sense of urgency or excitement. They make it easy for your audience to know exactly what to do next.

Examples:

- "Double-tap if you agree!"

- "Tag a friend who needs to see this!"

- "Share your thoughts in the comments below!"

- "Don't miss out—shop now!"

- "Limited time offer—sign up today!"

Why It's Effective: These CTAs encourage followers to interact, share, or make a purchase, thus increasing engagement rates.

Best Practices for Using CTAs:

Why It Works: The placement, clarity, and urgency of a CTA can directly impact its success.

> **Tip:** Place your CTA at the end of your caption for maximum impact, ensuring it stands out as the last thing your audience reads.

Example: "Ready to elevate your skincare routine? Shop now and get 15% off your first order—limited time only!"

> **Tip:** Be clear about the action you want your followers to take and use **action-oriented language** to create a sense of urgency.

Example: "Hurry, the sale ends soon—grab your favorite pieces today!"

Why It's Effective: A clear and specific CTA helps users understand exactly what you want them to do, while action-oriented language pushes them toward taking that action quickly.

Conclusion

Captions play an integral role in your social media strategy. A well-crafted caption grabs attention, fosters engagement, and drives specific actions from your audience. By starting with a strong hook, maintaining a conversational tone, and using hashtags wisely, you can ensure your captions resonate with your followers. Additionally, storytelling helps you connect on an emotional level, while user-generated content enhances trust and community-building. Finally, incorporating compelling **Call to Actions (CTAs)** can drive conversions and boost engagement. With these techniques, you'll be able to create captions that not only captivate but also inspire your audience to take meaningful action.

Creating engaging content is more than just posting pretty pictures and catchy captions. It involves understanding your audience, leveraging the right content mix, using powerful tools, and crafting messages that resonate. By applying the strategies outlined in this chapter, you'll be well on your way to boosting your social media presence and achieving your business goals. Remember, the key to success is consistency, creativity, and always putting your audience first.

Chapter 4: Building a Loyal Following

Establishing a loyal following on social media is essential for long-term success. Whether you're looking to increase brand awareness, boost engagement, or drive sales, building a strong community of followers who trust and support your brand is key. This chapter will guide you through organic growth strategies, paid social media tactics, and the power of influencer collaborations to help you build a devoted audience.

Growing Your Audience Organically

Growing your social media following organically may take time and consistent effort, but the benefits are significant in the long term. Organic growth focuses on attracting followers who genuinely resonate with your brand, which leads to higher engagement rates, a more loyal audience, and deeper customer relationships. Unlike paid ads, which may bring in temporary results, organic growth is a sustainable strategy that builds trust, credibility, and a community around your brand.

Best Practices for Gaining Followers Without Paid Ads

Optimize Your Profile:

Why It Works: Your profile is often the first impression users will have of your brand, so it's crucial to ensure it's inviting, informative, and clear.

> **Tip:**
>
> Complete your profile with essential elements such as a **clear bio**, a **high-quality profile photo**, and a **link to your website or landing page**. These elements tell users who you are, what you offer, and how they can connect with you.

Use **relevant keywords** in your bio to help your profile appear in search results when potential followers are looking for content related to your industry.

Include a **compelling Call to Action (CTA)** that prompts users to follow you, such as "Follow us for daily tips!" or "Join the community of creatives – follow us now!"

Why It's Effective: Optimizing your profile helps increase visibility and encourages users to follow and engage with your content.

Create Shareable Content:

Why It Works: The more shareable your content, the more likely it is to reach new people and expand your following.

Tip:

- Focus on creating **high-quality, valuable content** that resonates with your target audience. Content that educates, entertains, or inspires is more likely to be shared.
- Use a **variety of content types** to keep your feed dynamic. This can include **infographics, videos, memes, inspirational quotes**, or behind-the-scenes looks at your business.
- **Post consistently** to stay visible in your followers' feeds. Establish a posting schedule that aligns with your audience's activity patterns to maximize engagement.

Why It's Effective: Consistent, shareable content keeps your audience engaged and attracts new followers, as people are more likely to follow accounts that provide value.

Use Hashtags Strategically:

Why It Works: Hashtags make your content discoverable to users outside your current follower base, allowing you to reach a broader audience.

Tip:

- Research and use **popular, niche, and industry-specific hashtags** that align with your content. This can significantly increase your visibility and help attract followers who are genuinely interested in your brand.
- **Create a branded hashtag** that followers can use to share their own experiences with your products or services, helping to build a sense of community.

- Avoid using too many hashtags—**5-10 relevant hashtags** per post is a sweet spot that doesn't clutter your caption.

Why It's Effective: Well-chosen hashtags increase the discoverability of your posts and encourage user participation through branded hashtags.

Leveraging Community Engagement (Commenting, Sharing, Collaborating)

Engage with Your Followers:

Why It Works: Building strong relationships with your followers encourages loyalty, increases engagement, and boosts your visibility on social media.

Tip:

- **Respond promptly** to comments, direct messages, and mentions. A quick response shows followers that you care about their input and encourages more engagement.

- Ask **open-ended questions** in your captions to foster conversations. Engaging in dialogue with your audience makes them feel more connected to your brand.

- Show **appreciation** for your followers by liking and replying to their comments. This increases visibility and engagement, while also making your followers feel valued.

Why It's Effective: Engaging with your followers builds a loyal community and improves your position in social media algorithms, which prioritize content with higher engagement.

1. **Collaborate with Other Brands and Accounts:**

Why It Works: Collaboration can introduce your brand to a new audience, increasing your visibility and follower count in a natural, non-promotional way.

Tip:

- Partner with brands or influencers who share a similar target audience but are not direct competitors. For example, a fitness brand might collaborate with a nutritionist or healthy food brand.
- Co-hosting **Instagram Lives, Facebook events**, or **webinars** is a great way to reach new audiences while providing valuable content.
- **Engage with others in your industry** by commenting on their posts, sharing their content, or joining relevant online communities. These actions can help foster relationships and increase the likelihood of collaborations.

Why It's Effective: Collaborative efforts tap into new follower bases and position your brand as part of a larger, active community.

How to Host Social Media Contests and Giveaways

Benefits of Contests and Giveaways:

Why It Works: Contests and giveaways are powerful tools to attract new followers, increase engagement, and create excitement around your brand. They also provide a direct incentive for users to interact with your content.

Tip:

- Contests not only **grow your follower count** but can also help expand your **email list** or **drive traffic to your website** by requiring entrants to visit your site or sign up for newsletters.
- These events generate buzz around your products or services, making them more likely to be shared across social media platforms.

Best Practices for Running a Successful Contest:

Define Clear Goals: Before starting a contest, decide whether your primary goal is to **gain followers**, **boost engagement**, or **promote a specific product or service**. Your goals will influence the type of contest you run and how you measure success.

- **Example:** If you're looking to grow your follower base, ask users to follow your account, tag a friend, and like the post as entry requirements.

Choose an Attractive Prize: The prize should be appealing to your target audience and relevant to your brand. It could be a product from your store, a gift card, or a free service that showcases your expertise.

- **Example:** For a skincare brand, offering a free skincare consultation or a product bundle as a prize would be highly relevant to your followers.

Set Simple Rules: Make it easy for participants to enter. Complicated or confusing rules may discourage people from participating.

- **Example:** "To enter, simply follow us, like this post, and tag two friends who would love this!"

Promote Your Contest: Utilize **Instagram Stories, Facebook Groups, and email newsletters** to promote your contest. The more people know about it, the more likely you are to see an increase in engagement and followers.

Announce the Winner: After the contest ends, publicly announce the winner on your social media platforms to build credibility and excitement for future contests.

- **Example:** "Congratulations to @user_name for winning our giveaway! Stay tuned for more chances to win! 🎉 "

Why It's Effective: Contests and giveaways spark excitement, encourage sharing, and can help grow your audience quickly without the need for paid ads.

Conclusion

Organic growth on social media requires a combination of optimizing your profile, creating valuable content, engaging with your followers, and fostering collaboration. By focusing on these practices, you'll attract a loyal and engaged following that is genuinely interested in what you offer. Additionally, leveraging strategies such as community engagement, contests, and giveaways can further enhance your efforts, creating an interactive and enthusiastic audience that helps your brand grow organically over time. While it may take more effort than paid ads, the results are worth it in terms of stronger customer relationships and sustained success.

Paid Social Media Strategies

Paid social media strategies offer a fast track to grow your brand's presence, allowing you to reach a larger, more targeted audience. While organic growth focuses on attracting followers who naturally engage with your content, paid social media ads enable you to promote your message beyond your current followers. This approach provides businesses with powerful tools to expand their reach, boost conversions, and drive traffic. Below is an expanded guide on how to implement and optimize paid social media strategies for maximum effectiveness.

Overview of Paid Advertising on Facebook, Instagram, and LinkedIn

1. Facebook Ads:

- **Ad Formats:** Facebook offers various ad formats that cater to different marketing objectives. These include:

    - **Photo Ads:** Simple and effective, perfect for showcasing products or services.

    - **Video Ads:** Engaging and ideal for storytelling, demonstrating how your product works, or building brand awareness.

    - **Carousel Ads:** Multiple images or videos in a single ad, allowing you to showcase multiple products or services.

    - **Sponsored Posts:** These blend seamlessly into users' feeds and appear as part of the content they already engage with.

- **Targeting Options:** Facebook's sophisticated targeting options allow you to precisely define your audience. You can target based on:

  - Demographics (age, gender, education, etc.)

  - Interests (hobbies, lifestyle, etc.)

  - Behaviors (past purchase activity, device usage, etc.)

  - Custom audiences (based on email lists or website visitors).

2. Instagram Ads:

- **Ad Formats:** Instagram is highly visual, and its ad formats leverage this visual appeal:

  - **Photo Ads:** Showcase your products in a visually compelling way.

  - **Video Ads:** Short-form video content that captures users' attention.

  - **Instagram Stories Ads:** Full-screen, immersive ads that appear between user stories.

  - **Shoppable Posts:** Allow users to purchase directly from your post, ideal for e-commerce brands.

- **Targeting Features:** Instagram allows advertisers to use targeting based on:

  - User behaviors (likes, follows, previous interactions)

- o Interests (based on activity like posts they engage with).

3. LinkedIn Ads:

- **Ad Formats:** LinkedIn is the top platform for B2B marketing and offers ad formats including:

  - o **Sponsored Content:** Native ads that appear in the feed and look like regular posts.

  - o **Sponsored InMail:** Personalized messages sent directly to a user's inbox, effective for lead generation.

  - o **Text Ads:** Simple, concise ads that appear on the sidebars of LinkedIn pages.

- **Targeting Options:** LinkedIn's targeting is highly focused on professional attributes:

  - o Job titles, industries, company size, and professional interests.

  - o LinkedIn also allows you to upload a contact list and target users with specific skills or experiences, making it ideal for reaching decision-makers.

Setting Up Your First Ad Campaign: Targeting, Budgeting, and Ad Creatives

1. Define Your Campaign Objective:

Start by identifying the core objective of your campaign, as this will guide all your ad decisions. Facebook, Instagram, and LinkedIn all offer several campaign objectives to choose from:

- **Brand Awareness:** Increase visibility and reach.

- **Lead Generation:** Collect email addresses or other contact information.

- **Website Traffic:** Drive users to your site.

- **Conversions:** Encourage actions like purchases or form submissions.

2. Target the Right Audience:

Effective targeting is key to maximizing your ROI with paid social media ads. Take advantage of the advanced filtering tools available:

- **Demographic Filters:** Age, gender, location, education, etc.

- **Interest-Based Targeting:** Cater your ads to users based on their online behavior, such as previous searches or social media activities.

- **Custom Audiences:** Reach people who have interacted with your business previously, like website visitors or email subscribers.

- **Lookalike Audiences:** Identify and target users who share similar behaviors or characteristics to your existing audience, increasing the likelihood of engagement.

3. Set Your Budget and Schedule:

- **Budgeting:** You can choose between a daily or lifetime budget. A daily budget ensures you stay within a certain spend per day, while a lifetime budget allows you to spend a fixed amount over the course of the entire campaign.

- **Testing with Small Budgets:** It's often wise to start with a small budget to test how your ads perform before scaling up.

- **Scheduling:** Align your ad schedule with the times when your target audience is most active. This will help ensure your ads reach the right people at the right time.

4. Create Compelling Ad Creatives:

Your ad creatives (images, videos, and copy) are the face of your campaign. To create ads that stand out:

- **Visual Appeal:** Use high-quality, eye-catching visuals that reflect your brand identity.

- **Engaging Copy:** Write concise, persuasive text that speaks directly to your audience's needs or pain points. A strong value proposition is key.

- **Clear CTA:** Include a compelling call-to-action (CTA) such as "Shop Now," "Sign Up," or "Learn More," directing users to take the next step.

Measuring the ROI of Your Social Media Ads

1. Track Key Metrics:

Once your campaign is live, you'll need to track performance. Key metrics to monitor include:

- **Click-Through Rate (CTR):** Measures how often people click on your ad after seeing it.

- **Cost Per Click (CPC):** The average cost you pay each time someone clicks on your ad.

- **Cost Per Acquisition (CPA):** The cost you incur for each conversion, such as a purchase or sign-up.

- **Return on Ad Spend (ROAS):** Measures how much revenue you generate for each dollar spent on ads.

2. Optimize Your Campaigns:

Constant optimization is crucial to improving your ad performance:

- **A/B Testing:** Test different ad creatives, copy, and CTAs to identify what resonates best with your audience. For example, try different headlines, images, or offers to see which generates the highest engagement.

- **Refining Targeting:** Monitor which audience segments are performing best and adjust your targeting accordingly. For example, you may find that your ads perform better with a specific age group or interest category, allowing you to narrow your focus for better results.

- **Budget Adjustments:** Based on the performance of your ads, you can increase or decrease your budget to allocate more spend toward high-performing campaigns.

Paid social media ads, when implemented correctly, can fast-track your brand's growth, increase engagement, and drive conversions. However, continuous optimization and understanding the nuances of each platform's targeting and ad formats are critical to achieving the best ROI. By aligning your objectives, targeting the right audience, and monitoring key metrics, you'll be able to scale your paid social campaigns with confidence.

Influencer Partnerships and Collaborations

Influencer marketing is a powerful tool that can significantly boost your brand's reach, build trust, and increase conversions. By partnering with influencers, you tap into an audience that already trusts their recommendations, which can make your products or services more appealing to potential customers. Since influencers have established relationships with their followers, their endorsements carry more weight than traditional advertising. This section explores how to effectively work with influencers to enhance your brand's visibility and drive meaningful results.

Finding and Reaching Out to Influencers

1. Identify the Right Influencers:

Choosing the right influencer is crucial for the success of your campaign. Here's how to select influencers who will effectively promote your brand:

- **Audience Alignment:** Ensure that the influencer's followers align with your target market. For instance, if you're marketing a health supplement, seek influencers in the health, wellness, and fitness niches.

- **Niche Relevance:** Evaluate the influencer's specific niche (e.g., beauty, travel, food, tech) and how well it matches your brand's offerings.

- **Follower Count and Engagement Rate:** While a large follower count can indicate broad reach, engagement rate (the level of interaction their followers have with their content) is often a better indicator of an influencer's ability to drive action. Micro-influencers with smaller but highly engaged audiences can be just as valuable as larger influencers.

- **Content Style:** Analyze the influencer's content style to see if it resonates with your brand's tone and image. An influencer whose content feels authentic and relatable is more likely to produce genuine results.

To streamline the process, platforms like **Upfluence**, **AspireIQ**, and **HypeAuditor** offer tools to help you discover influencers who align with your brand values and audience demographics. These platforms also provide valuable metrics on influencer performance, making it easier to gauge their effectiveness before reaching out.

2. Craft a Personalized Outreach Message:

Once you've identified the right influencer, it's time to reach out. A generic or overly sales-driven message may come off as insincere. Instead, personalize your outreach:

- **Personalization:** Mention specific aspects of their content that you admire or how their style aligns with your brand's ethos. This demonstrates that you've taken the time to research and understand their influence.

- **Clear Benefits for Both Parties:** Highlight what the influencer will gain from the partnership. Whether it's free products, exclusive discounts for their followers, or monetary compensation, make sure the influencer sees clear value in working with your brand.

- **Professionalism and Respect:** Treat influencers as business partners, and approach the conversation with respect for their time and audience. This helps build a long-term, mutually beneficial relationship.

3. Offer Creative Freedom:

One of the key components of successful influencer partnerships is allowing influencers the creative freedom to represent your brand in a way that feels authentic to them. Influencers know their audience better than anyone else, so let them showcase your product or service in a manner that resonates with their followers.

- **Avoid Micromanaging:** Giving influencers the space to create content their followers will enjoy leads to more organic, believable endorsements. Forcing them to follow rigid guidelines can feel inauthentic and harm the partnership.

- **Authenticity is Key:** Influencers build trust by being genuine with their followers. Allowing them to speak naturally about your brand will result in more relatable and successful campaigns.

Best Practices for Working with Influencers to Expand Your Reach

1. Set Clear Expectations:

Clear communication from the outset is vital to ensure the success of your influencer collaboration. Establish the following points early on:

- **Goals and Deliverables:** Define what success looks like for both parties, whether it's an increase in website traffic, product sales, or brand awareness.

- **Compensation Details:** Whether the influencer will be paid, receive free products, or earn affiliate commissions, establish the compensation terms upfront to avoid confusion.

- **Timelines:** Set a clear timeline for deliverables, including when the content should be posted and any key dates for promotions or product launches.

- **Brand Guidelines:** Share essential brand guidelines, including tone of voice, key messages, and any do's and don'ts for the collaboration. However, remember to balance this with creative freedom.

2. Leverage Different Types of Collaborations:

There are several ways to collaborate with influencers that can yield different results:

- **Sponsored Posts:** Pay influencers to create posts featuring your products or services. These can be either Instagram posts, YouTube videos, or blog articles, depending on the platform.

- **Giveaways:** Hosting a giveaway can be an excellent way to boost engagement and increase followers. This collaboration can be structured to require participants to follow both your account and the influencer's, tag friends, or engage with a specific piece of content.

- **Affiliate Marketing:** Offer influencers a commission for every sale generated through their unique affiliate link. This is an incentive-based model that encourages influencers to promote your product more actively.

- **Product Reviews or Unboxings:** Sending influencers your product and asking them to share their genuine feedback can be a powerful way to build trust and interest among their followers.

3. Monitor the Performance of Influencer Campaigns:

Once your influencer campaign is live, it's important to track its success. Here are some key metrics to focus on:

- **Engagement Rate:** The level of interaction (likes, comments, shares) the influencer's content receives. This is a direct measure of how well the content resonates with their audience.

- **Reach and Impressions:** Monitor how many people saw the influencer's content and how many of them engaged with it. This gives you an idea of the campaign's overall visibility.

- **Conversion Rate:** Track how many people take the desired action (such as purchasing a product or signing up for a newsletter) after interacting with the influencer's content.

Utilize **custom discount codes, tracking links,** or **UTM parameters** to track the sales and traffic that come from influencer campaigns. These tools help you measure the effectiveness of your partnerships and determine which influencers are delivering the best results.

How to Track the Success of Influencer Campaigns

1. Use Analytics Tools:

There are several tools available to track the success of your influencer campaigns:

- **Google Analytics:** Track website traffic driven by influencer links or campaigns.

- **Social Media Insights:** Platforms like Instagram, Facebook, and Twitter provide insights into engagement, reach, and impressions. These metrics can help you understand how well an influencer's post is performing.

- **Bitly Links:** Use custom shortened links to track click-through rates from influencer posts.

By comparing the metrics from your influencer campaigns against your overall marketing goals, you can gauge the success of your efforts. This will allow you to refine your strategy for future campaigns and optimize your return on investment.

2. Collect Feedback from Influencers:

After the campaign concludes, gather feedback from the influencers themselves:

- **What Worked:** Ask them about what elements of the collaboration worked well and which tactics drove the most engagement.

- **Opportunities for Improvement:** Request suggestions on how the collaboration process can be improved for both parties in the future.

This feedback will provide valuable insights into what resonated with the influencer's audience and help you refine your approach to influencer partnerships going forward.

Incorporating influencer partnerships into your marketing strategy can lead to more authentic and expansive brand promotion. By selecting the right influencers, setting clear expectations, and monitoring campaign performance, you can build long-lasting relationships that not only drive brand awareness but also directly contribute to sales and customer loyalty.

Conclusion

Building a loyal social media following requires a combination of organic growth strategies, paid advertising, and influencer collaborations. By engaging with your audience, leveraging the power of social media ads, and partnering with influencers, you can expand your reach, increase brand awareness, and build lasting relationships with your followers. The key to success is consistency, authenticity, and always putting your audience's needs first. With the strategies outlined in this chapter, you'll be well on your way to creating a devoted, engaged community around your brand.

Chapter 5: Driving Engagement and Building Community

Engagement is the lifeblood of social media marketing. While growing your follower count is important, it is the level of interaction you foster with your audience that determines the true success of your social media presence. This chapter explores why engagement is so important, effective strategies to boost engagement, and how you can build a loyal community around your brand.

The Importance of Engagement

Social media has rapidly evolved from a platform for simple status updates and photos to a dynamic, interactive ecosystem where success is defined not just by the number of followers but by the quality of interactions your audience has with your content. Engagement—measured through likes, comments, shares, clicks, and other forms of interaction—has become the true benchmark for assessing the effectiveness of social media strategies. In this section, we will explore why engagement is the key to social media success and how it can drive visibility, build relationships, and ultimately lead to greater business success.

Why Engagement Matters More Than Follower Count

While the number of followers you have can give you a rough idea of your reach, it's not necessarily indicative of the success or influence of your brand. Engagement—meaning the active involvement of your audience with your posts—holds far more weight when it comes to determining your social media impact.

1. Quality Over Quantity:

- **Smaller, Engaged Audiences Are More Valuable:** A smaller, highly engaged audience is often far more valuable than a large, passive one. This is because engaged followers are more likely to take meaningful actions, such as purchasing your products, sharing your content, or recommending your brand to others. A brand with a deep connection to its audience is more likely to foster loyalty and generate word-of-mouth marketing.

- **Engagement Drives Visibility:** Social media platforms are designed to promote content that gets interaction. When users engage with your posts, it signals to the platform that your content is valuable. This can result in your content being shown to more users, often beyond just your followers, expanding your reach organically.

- **Building a Loyal Audience:** While having a large following can be beneficial, it is engagement that truly nurtures relationships. An engaged audience is more likely to become repeat customers and brand advocates. They feel valued when they interact with your posts, which encourages further interaction and, over time, builds loyalty.

2. Building Relationships:

- **Direct Interaction and Customer Connection:** Social media isn't just a tool for broadcasting your brand; it's an opportunity to create genuine, two-way conversations. Engaging with your followers allows you to answer their questions, address concerns, and make them feel heard and valued. These interactions foster a sense of community and allow you to build stronger, more personal relationships with your audience.

- **Trust and Loyalty:** Engagement is essential for building trust. By consistently responding to comments, liking posts, and engaging in meaningful conversations, you show that you care about your audience's thoughts and needs. This trust is vital for turning followers into customers, advocates, and long-term brand loyalists who will support your business even beyond initial purchases.

The Social Media Algorithms and How Engagement Impacts Visibility

Social media platforms use complex algorithms to decide what content appears in users' feeds. These algorithms prioritize posts that spark engagement, and the more engagement your content receives, the more likely it is to be seen by a larger audience. Let's break down how engagement directly impacts visibility on some of the most popular platforms.

1. Facebook and Instagram:

- **Engagement as a Ranking Factor:** Both Facebook and Instagram rely on engagement signals to rank posts in users' feeds. The more likes, comments, shares, and other interactions a post receives, the higher it ranks in the feed. This means that posts with high engagement are more likely to be seen by both followers and non-followers.

- **The Power of Comments and Shares:** While likes are important, comments and shares hold more weight in the algorithms. Comments signify that users are interacting with your content in a more meaningful way, while shares indicate that users find your content valuable enough to pass it along to others. The more comments and shares your post gets, the more likely it is to be shown to new people.

2. LinkedIn:

- **Focus on Professional Engagement:** LinkedIn's algorithm values engagement, but it places a greater emphasis on meaningful interactions like comments and shares within professional circles. As LinkedIn is a platform built around networking and professional growth, engagement on LinkedIn can help you foster relationships, build authority, and position yourself as a thought leader in your industry.

- **B2B Implications:** For businesses that target other businesses (B2B), engagement on LinkedIn can be especially valuable. Regular, thoughtful engagement with posts not only boosts your visibility within your network but also helps you build connections that can lead to new business opportunities, partnerships, or collaborations.

3. Twitter:

- **Real-Time Engagement and Relevancy:** On Twitter, engagement is all about real-time conversations. The platform's fast-paced nature means that tweets with frequent interactions—such as retweets, replies, and likes—are more likely to be seen by a broader audience, especially during trending topics or live events.

- **Hashtags and Trending Topics:** Hashtags play a big role in the Twitter algorithm, as they categorize content and increase its visibility. By engaging with trending topics or relevant hashtags, you can boost the reach of your tweets and engage with a larger audience who may be interested in your content.

4. TikTok:

- **Viral Potential of Engagement:** TikTok's algorithm is highly engagement-driven. The platform prioritizes content that receives likes, comments, shares, and video completions. The more engagement a video receives, the more likely it is to appear on the "For You" page, increasing the chances of the video going viral and reaching millions of users. TikTok's success lies in its ability to surface content that resonates with users, based on engagement and relevance, rather than just follower count.

How Engagement Affects Your Social Media Strategy

- **Boosts Organic Reach:** Higher engagement leads to better organic reach. The more people interact with your content, the more likely it is to appear in the feeds of others, potentially leading to new followers and customers.

- **Increases Conversions:** Engaged audiences are more likely to take action—whether that's clicking a link, signing up for a newsletter, or making a purchase. The more engaged your followers are, the higher the chances they'll convert into paying customers.

- **Improves Brand Perception:** Consistent engagement with your followers shows that your brand is accessible, responsive, and authentic. This fosters a positive brand image and enhances customer loyalty, which is essential for long-term success.

- **Provides Insights for Content Creation:** By tracking engagement metrics, you can identify what types of content resonate most with your audience. This insight allows you to refine your content strategy to produce more of what your followers love, keeping them engaged and increasing the likelihood of sharing your posts with others.

Conclusion: Engagement is Key to Social Media Success

In the current social media landscape, engagement is far more important than follower count. While followers can be an indicator of your reach, it's the interactions with your audience that truly determine the success of your social media efforts. By focusing on building genuine relationships, creating engaging content, and fostering active conversations with your followers, you can increase your visibility, build trust, and drive conversions. Ultimately, a well-engaged audience will not only help amplify your content but also support your brand long-term, making engagement the cornerstone of any successful social media strategy.

Strategies to Boost Engagement

Driving engagement on social media requires more than just posting content—it's about creating opportunities for interaction and fostering relationships with your audience. The goal is to make your followers feel involved, heard, and valued. By employing a variety of strategies that invite participation, you can turn passive followers into active brand advocates. Here are some powerful strategies to boost engagement across your social media platforms.

Creating Interactive Content (Polls, Quizzes, Q&A Sessions)

Interactive content is a great way to get your audience involved. It sparks curiosity, encourages participation, and can even provide valuable feedback or insights. Here are three types of interactive content to integrate into your social media strategy:

1. Polls and Surveys:

- **Quick and Engaging Participation:** Polls are one of the easiest ways to get your audience to engage. Platforms like Instagram Stories, Facebook, and Twitter make it simple for users to vote on a question with a tap or click. Polls are effective because they require minimal effort, making it easy for your audience to participate.

- **Ask Questions That Spark Curiosity or Offer Value:** Use polls to ask questions that resonate with your followers or are directly tied to your business. For instance, "What product would you love to see us introduce next?" or "Which of these tips helped you the most?" These questions not only encourage interaction but also give you insight into your audience's preferences, which can inform your future content strategy.

- **Gain Insight and Drive Action:** You can also use polls to test out new ideas, understand pain points, or get feedback on services. Polls are a great way to collect valuable information while keeping the conversation light and fun.

2. Quizzes:

- **Engaging and Fun Learning Opportunities:** Quizzes can be both entertaining and educational for your audience. Creating a quiz related to your industry or product can spark interest and give your followers something to look forward to. For example, if you sell beauty products, you might offer a quiz to help your followers find their ideal skincare routine.

- **Personalized Results for Deeper Connection:** Quizzes that provide personalized results can be especially engaging. Offering tailored recommendations or insights based on quiz outcomes makes the experience more memorable and relevant to your audience.

- **Gather Audience Data for Future Content:** Quizzes are also an excellent way to collect data about your followers' preferences, habits, or knowledge of your brand. The answers they provide can guide future content creation, product offerings, and marketing strategies.

3. Q&A Sessions:

- **Real-Time Interaction with Followers:** Hosting Q&A sessions is an excellent way to interact with your audience directly. Use platforms like Instagram Stories, Facebook Live, or LinkedIn to answer questions from your followers in real-time. This not only fosters a sense of community but also shows your audience that you're accessible and willing to engage with them personally.

- **Engage with Topics That Matter:** Choose topics that your audience cares about. You can focus on your products, services, or broader industry-related subjects. By addressing the things that matter most to your followers, you demonstrate that you understand their needs.

- **Create Anticipation for Future Sessions:** If you schedule Q&A sessions regularly, you'll create anticipation. Your followers will look forward to these sessions and may start submitting questions ahead of time, increasing their engagement and involvement with your brand.

The Power of Live Video: Hosting Live Streams, Webinars, and AMAs (Ask Me Anything)

Live video has emerged as one of the most effective forms of content for boosting engagement. Whether through live streams, webinars, or AMAs, live content offers a sense of real-time connection that pre-recorded content cannot match. Here are three live video strategies to boost engagement:

1. Live Streams:

- **Connect Authentically with Your Audience:** Live streams are an incredible way to connect with your audience on a deeper level. Whether you're hosting a product launch, sharing behind-the-scenes footage, or having an informal chat with your followers, live video allows for unfiltered, real-time communication. The spontaneity of live streaming fosters an authentic and personal connection that your followers will appreciate.

- **Real-Time Interaction:** One of the greatest advantages of live video is the ability to respond to questions and comments as they come in. This interactive aspect of live streaming creates a more dynamic and engaging experience, allowing your audience to feel involved in the conversation.

- **Boost Visibility and Reach:** Platforms like Instagram, Facebook, and LinkedIn all prioritize live content in users' feeds. This means that live video can help you boost visibility and reach more people organically.

2. Webinars:

- **Provide Valuable, In-Depth Content:** Webinars offer a great way to dive deep into a subject that interests your audience. Whether you're providing product education, sharing industry insights, or hosting a skills development session, webinars allow you to engage with your followers in a structured, informative way.

- **Engage Through Polls and Chats:** Webinars allow for real-time interaction through features like live polls, Q&A chats, and audience feedback. These interactive elements keep attendees engaged and make the experience more participatory.

- **Offer Incentives for Participation:** To encourage attendance and participation, offer exclusive benefits like free resources, discounts, or insider insights. This not only boosts engagement but also increases the perceived value of the webinar.

3. AMAs (Ask Me Anything):

- **Offer Direct Access to Your Expertise:** AMAs, especially on platforms like Reddit, Instagram, and Twitter, allow your followers to ask questions directly. This type of informal, real-time interaction helps humanize your brand and fosters a stronger bond with your community.

- **Promote Engagement with Exclusive Content:** Promote your AMA in advance to build anticipation and excitement. Encourage followers to submit questions beforehand to increase participation and engagement during the live session.

- **Create a Fun, Casual Experience:** AMAs are an excellent opportunity to show the lighter side of your brand and engage with your audience in a fun and casual manner. This informal setting can help build relationships and increase trust with your followers.

Encouraging User-Generated Content (UGC) and Sharing Customer Testimonials

User-generated content (UGC) and customer testimonials not only provide social proof but also create opportunities for authentic engagement. By encouraging your audience to contribute content, you build trust and foster a sense of community.

1. User-Generated Content (UGC):

- **Build Community and Trust:** UGC is one of the most authentic ways to engage your audience. Encourage your followers to share their experiences with your products or services by posting photos, videos, or reviews. This not only increases engagement but also shows your customers that their contributions are valued.

- **Repost UGC to Show Appreciation:** Sharing UGC on your social media platforms is a great way to acknowledge and appreciate your community. Reposting user-generated photos or videos makes your followers feel seen and appreciated, which strengthens their loyalty and encourages others to contribute as well.

- **Host UGC Campaigns:** Run campaigns or contests where users can submit content related to your brand. For example, you can ask customers to post a photo of themselves using your product with a branded hashtag for a chance to win a prize. This increases engagement while promoting your brand.

2. Customer Testimonials:

- **Leverage Social Proof to Build Credibility:** Sharing customer testimonials and success stories is an effective way to showcase the value of your products or services. Positive reviews, especially when shared by real customers, build credibility and trust with your audience.

- **Turn Testimonials into Engaging Visual Content:** To make customer testimonials even more engaging, consider turning them into visual content like video testimonials, quote graphics, or short stories. Visual content is more likely to be shared and consumed, making it a great way to boost engagement.

- **Encourage Followers to Share Their Stories:** Ask your customers to share their own experiences with your products or services. This not only generates more user content but also increases engagement by creating a community of brand advocates who are excited to share their stories.

Conclusion: Engaging Your Audience is Key to Social Media Success

Boosting engagement on social media requires a strategic approach that combines interactive content, live experiences, and user-generated contributions. By creating opportunities for your audience to interact with your brand, you foster deeper connections, build trust, and increase visibility. Whether through polls, live videos, AMAs, or sharing customer testimonials, the key to success is making your audience feel involved and valued. Implement these strategies consistently, and you'll see increased engagement, improved brand loyalty, and a stronger online presence.

Building a Community Around Your Brand

A loyal community isn't just about high engagement; it's about creating a space where followers feel valued, heard, and part of something bigger. Building a strong community around your brand can lead to long-term customer retention, advocacy, and organic growth.

How to Create and Manage Facebook Groups and LinkedIn Communities

1. Facebook Groups:

Facebook Groups offer a unique opportunity to connect people with shared interests, experiences, or professional backgrounds. By creating a Facebook Group for your brand, you can build a space where members feel a sense of belonging, engage in meaningful discussions, and access exclusive content.

Best Practices for Facebook Groups:

- **Set Clear Rules and Guidelines:** Establish rules to ensure respectful, constructive, and valuable conversations. Guidelines help manage group dynamics and keep the community safe.

- **Post Regularly with Valuable Content:** Keep your group engaged by sharing valuable insights, updates, and resources. However, don't just post your own content—encourage group members to share their thoughts and experiences.

- **Encourage User-Generated Content:** Use polls, discussions, and live Q&A sessions to foster more interaction. Encourage members to post content, share their knowledge, and connect with one another.

2. LinkedIn Communities:

LinkedIn Groups (now integrated as LinkedIn Communities) are an excellent option for B2B brands. They provide a space to network with industry professionals, share knowledge, and establish your brand as an authority within your field.

Best Practices for LinkedIn Communities:

- **Focus on Knowledge Sharing:** Create a community where professionals can learn, share insights, and exchange ideas. The emphasis should be on adding value and facilitating meaningful conversations.

- **Post Thoughtful Content:** Post valuable and industry-relevant content that sparks discussions and encourages engagement. Encourage members to interact with each other by asking thought-provoking questions and offering unique perspectives.

The Role of Community Management in Customer Retention

1. Engage with Your Community Regularly:

Consistency is key when managing a community. Regular engagement ensures that your followers feel valued and heard, which helps to strengthen your relationship with them.

- **Respond Promptly:** Reply to comments, messages, and posts to show your followers that their opinions and contributions matter. Even if you can't respond immediately, acknowledging them as soon as possible is essential.

- **Use Community Management Tools:** Tools like Sprout Social, Buffer, and Hootsuite allow you to track interactions and conversations across different social platforms. By staying on top of your communications, you can quickly respond to feedback, questions, and concerns.

2. Create a Two-Way Communication Channel:

Community management is a two-way street. It's not just about broadcasting content—it's about creating a dialogue between you and your followers.

- **Encourage Feedback and Questions:** Make it easy for your audience to share their thoughts, ask questions, and give feedback. This shows them that their voice matters and helps you create content or products that better meet their needs.

- **Respond with Personalization:** Whenever possible, tailor your responses to each individual. Personalized replies help deepen relationships and make your community members feel seen and heard.

Responding to Comments, Messages, and Reviews Effectively

1. Comments:

Engaging with comments is one of the most straightforward ways to maintain an active community. Show appreciation for positive comments and thoughtfully address any concerns or questions.

- **Acknowledge Compliments:** Always thank users for their positive feedback and let them know how much you value their support.

- **Handle Negative Comments Professionally:** Negative comments can be tricky, but they are an opportunity to demonstrate your professionalism. Respond empathetically, offer solutions, and ensure that the commenter feels heard and respected.

2. Messages:

Direct messages offer a more personal form of communication with your followers, helping to nurture relationships.

- **Respond Quickly and Helpfully:** Timely responses to DMs help build trust and ensure that your community members feel supported.

- **Offer Personalized Interactions:** Whether you're answering questions, offering product recommendations, or sharing exclusive offers, personalized responses make your followers feel special and valued.

3. Reviews:

Responding to reviews—whether positive or negative—helps reinforce your brand's commitment to customer satisfaction and shows that you value feedback.

- **Thank Positive Reviewers:** Express gratitude for customers who leave positive reviews, and let them know how much you appreciate their support. Sharing their testimonial on your social media or website is also a great way to celebrate your community.

- **Address Negative Reviews Constructively:** When responding to negative reviews, take a calm and solution-oriented approach. Acknowledge the issue, apologize if necessary, and offer steps to resolve the problem. Turning a negative experience into a positive one can deepen customer loyalty.

By implementing these strategies, you can build a vibrant community that not only supports your brand but also advocates for it, fostering long-term relationships and driving organic growth.

Conclusion

Engagement and community building are essential to thriving on social media. It's not just about gaining followers—it's about fostering meaningful relationships that lead to brand loyalty, advocacy, and organic growth. By implementing strategies like creating interactive content, leveraging live video, encouraging user-generated content, and effectively managing your social media communities, you can build a vibrant, engaged following that supports your brand long-term.

Chapter 6: Measuring and Analyzing Your Social Media Performance

In the fast-paced world of social media, measuring and analyzing your performance is essential to ensuring your strategies are effective. Without insights into how your content is performing, it's impossible to know what's working, what isn't, and where you should focus your efforts for improvement. This chapter delves into the key social media metrics you should track, how to create meaningful reports, and the power of A/B testing to fine-tune your approach.

Key Social Media Metrics to Track

Understanding social media metrics is essential for optimizing your strategy and achieving your goals. The metrics you track will give you valuable insights into what content resonates with your audience, how your campaigns are performing, and areas where you can improve. Here are the key metrics you should focus on to measure your success and refine your approach:

Understanding Metrics: Engagement Rate, Reach, Impressions, Conversion Rate

1. Engagement Rate:

The engagement rate is a crucial metric that measures how much your audience interacts with your content. It includes likes, comments, shares, and other forms of direct interaction. A high engagement rate indicates that your audience is actively involved with your brand, making it a strong indicator of brand affinity and interest.

How to Calculate Engagement Rate:

$$\text{Engagement Rate} = \frac{\text{Total Engagements}}{\text{Total Followers}} \times 100$$

This formula allows you to calculate the percentage of your audience who engages with your content compared to your total follower count.

Why It's Important:

- **Quality Over Quantity:** Engagement rate is often more valuable than simply tracking follower count. While having many followers is good, engagement rate demonstrates the depth of connection between your brand and its audience.

- **Content Optimization:** By tracking engagement, you can identify the types of posts that generate the most interaction. This allows you to create more content that your audience finds appealing, ultimately boosting your overall engagement.

2. Reach:

Reach refers to the total number of unique users who have seen your post. Unlike impressions, which measure total views, reach tracks the number of individual users who have been exposed to your content.

Why It's Important:

- **Audience Growth:** Reach helps you understand the size of your audience. If your reach is growing, it indicates that your content is being exposed to a wider audience, signaling the effectiveness of your social media strategy in increasing visibility.

- **Brand Awareness:** Tracking reach gives you insights into how many people are discovering your brand and content for the first time, which is especially important for building brand awareness.

3. Impressions:

Impressions measure how many times your content is displayed on a user's screen. This can be more than once per user, depending on how often they see your posts. It's a broader measure of exposure than reach because it counts all views, not just unique users.

Why It's Important:

- **Exposure and Visibility:** Impressions show how frequently your content is being seen. A higher number of impressions suggests your content is being widely circulated across platforms.

- **Identifying Engagement Opportunities:** If you notice a high number of impressions but a low engagement rate, it could suggest that while your content is visible, it isn't compelling enough to prompt interaction. This signals a need to optimize content or call-to-action elements.

4. Conversion Rate:

The conversion rate tracks the percentage of users who take a desired action after interacting with your content. This could include actions like making a purchase, signing up for a newsletter, or filling out a contact form. Conversion is a critical metric for evaluating the effectiveness of your social media marketing efforts.

How to Calculate Conversion Rate:

$$\text{Conversion Rate} = \frac{\text{Conversions}}{\text{Total Clicks or Interactions}} \times 100$$

This formula helps you determine how many users who clicked on your content went on to complete a desired action.

Why It's Important:

- **Effectiveness of Content:** Conversion rate is one of the most important metrics for assessing the real impact of your social media strategy. It helps you understand how well you are turning engagement into actual outcomes like sales or sign-ups.

- **Strategy Refinement:** Monitoring conversion rates helps you adjust your approach by identifying what types of content, campaigns, or messaging are most successful in driving action.

Setting Up Social Media Analytics Tools

Once you understand which metrics are important to track, the next step is to implement the right tools to measure them effectively. Fortunately, most major social media platforms offer built-in analytics tools that make it easy to track key metrics. Here's how to make the most of these tools:

1. Facebook Insights:

Facebook Insights is a powerful tool that allows you to track the performance of your Facebook content. It provides data on engagement, reach, impressions, and other key metrics. Whether you're posting organically or running paid campaigns, Facebook Insights allows you to analyze the performance of both types of posts.

What You Can Track:

- Engagement metrics like likes, comments, shares, and reactions.

- Reach and impressions for both organic and paid posts.

- Audience demographics, including location, age, and interests, helping you understand who your audience is.

- Best times to post based on when your audience is most active.

2. Instagram Insights:

Instagram Insights is an analytics tool designed to give you valuable data about your Instagram posts, stories, and overall account performance. The tool provides information about engagement, reach, impressions, and audience demographics.

What You Can Track:

- Engagement rate for posts, stories, and reels.

- Impressions and reach for individual posts and stories.

- Demographic insights, including age, gender, and location of your followers.

- Content performance by type, so you can see which types of posts (photos, videos, carousels, stories) generate the most engagement.

3. LinkedIn Analytics:

LinkedIn Analytics offers in-depth data on how your content performs within the professional landscape. It provides insights into your audience's engagement, your posts' reach, and the demographic characteristics of your followers.

What You Can Track:

- Post performance metrics, including views, shares, comments, and engagement rates.
- Audience insights, such as job title, industry, company size, and location.
- Conversion metrics, including clicks to your website or landing pages.
- Best times to post based on audience activity.

By regularly reviewing these analytics tools, you can gain valuable insights into how your social media content is performing. This data-driven approach will enable you to continuously refine your social media strategy, ensuring that you're meeting your business objectives and engaging effectively with your audience.

Creating Social Media Reports

Tracking metrics is essential, but the true value of your social media efforts lies in how you analyze, report, and use that data. By creating structured social media reports, you can assess your performance, refine your strategies, and effectively communicate the results of your social media campaigns to stakeholders.

How to Generate and Interpret Monthly/Quarterly Reports

1. **Set Up a Reporting Template**:

   - To streamline your reporting process, create a template using tools like Google Sheets, Excel, or specialized software such as Sprout Social, Hootsuite, or Buffer. A well-structured template ensures consistency and saves time.

   - Your report should include key metrics such as **engagement**, **reach**, **impressions**, and **conversion rate** for each platform. Include additional metrics such as **click-through rate** (CTR) or **video views** depending on the content type.

   - **Post-Level Breakdown**: Analyze individual post performance to identify which specific content types are resonating with your audience. This allows for a more granular understanding of what works and what doesn't.

2. **Monthly Reports**:

Monthly reports help you track short-term changes and make adjustments to your strategy quickly. These reports are valuable for identifying patterns in user behavior, such as optimal times to post, and the effectiveness of recent campaigns.

Focus Areas for Monthly Reports:

- **Growth in followers or engagement**: Look for month-over-month growth in these areas. High engagement indicates that your audience is interacting with your content, while increased followers show you're reaching more people.

- **High-performing content**: Identify which types of posts (e.g., videos, infographics, blog links) are generating the most engagement, and explore the effectiveness of specific **hashtags** or **calls to action**.

- **Paid ad performance**: If running ads, assess the performance of your paid campaigns. Analyze CTR, cost per click (CPC), and the return on ad spend (ROAS) to measure effectiveness.

3. **Quarterly Reports:**

Quarterly reports provide a broader view of your social media performance over a three-month period. These reports are useful for identifying larger trends, evaluating if your social media strategy aligns with broader business goals, and assessing ROI on a larger scale.

Focus Areas for Quarterly Reports:

- **Trends in follower growth, engagement, and conversions**: Look for consistent growth patterns. Are your followers engaging with your content more each quarter? Are conversions increasing as a result of social media efforts?

- **ROI on paid ads**: Review the effectiveness of any paid ad campaigns over the quarter, adjusting for changes in market conditions or audience behaviors.

- **Changes in audience demographics or behavior**: Quarterly reports are ideal for tracking shifts in who your audience is, such as changes in age, location, or interests, and adapting your strategy accordingly.

Using Data to Refine Your Social Media Strategy

The real value in creating social media reports lies in how you interpret the data and adjust your strategy based on those insights. Here's how to take action on your findings:

1. **Optimize Content Strategy**:

   - **Focus on High-Performing Content**: If certain types of content—such as **videos**, **polls**, or **carousel posts**—are consistently driving high engagement, prioritize those formats in your future posts.

   - **Content Type Adjustments**: Based on what resonates most with your audience, you might decide to increase the frequency of particular content types (e.g., more behind-the-scenes posts or tutorials).

   - **Refine Messaging**: Engagement data can reveal the messaging that your audience finds most compelling, whether it's humor, educational content, or user-generated stories.

2. **Adjust Posting Schedule**:

- Analyze engagement data to determine the **best days and times** to post. Social media platforms like Instagram, Facebook, and LinkedIn provide insights on when your audience is most active.

- **Optimal Scheduling Tools**: Use social media scheduling tools like **Later, Buffer,** or **Hootsuite** to plan and schedule your posts to go live at the times when your audience is most likely to engage. This can help you maximize reach and engagement.

3. **Refine Paid Ads**:

   - **Targeting Adjustments**: Social media ads provide valuable data on which demographics engage with your ads the most. If you notice certain age groups, genders, or interests perform better, adjust your targeting accordingly.

   - **Ad Budget Allocation**: Allocate your ad budget based on performance. If one particular ad or demographic group is outperforming others, increase the spend for that group while reducing spending on underperforming segments.

   - **Ad Creative Tweaks**: Based on your findings, refine your ad creatives, including imagery, copy, and calls to action. If one version of your ad performs better than others, replicate those elements in future campaigns.

4. **Set New Goals**:

   - Based on the insights from your reports, set **new Key Performance Indicators (KPIs)** for the upcoming month or quarter. For example, if engagement rates have plateaued, set a goal to increase engagement by a certain percentage.

- **Revise Underperforming Goals**: If you find that you're not meeting specific goals, like conversions or engagement rates, analyze the data to determine why, and adjust your strategy. Perhaps you need more targeted content, better calls to action, or revised ad targeting.

- **Celebrate Success**: Don't forget to celebrate milestones like reaching a specific number of followers or achieving a record number of conversions, which can boost team morale and help solidify the importance of social media efforts in your overall business strategy.

By consistently tracking, interpreting, and refining your social media reports, you can continuously improve your content strategy, engage your audience more effectively, and demonstrate the tangible value of social media to stakeholders.

A/B Testing for Better Results

A/B testing, also known as **split testing**, is a powerful method for optimizing your social media strategy and improving the effectiveness of your campaigns. By testing different elements within your social media content, posting schedule, and ad creatives, you can pinpoint what resonates most with your audience, allowing you to make data-driven decisions that maximize engagement and conversions.

The Importance of Testing Different Types of Content, Posting Times, and Ad Creatives

1. **Testing Content Formats:**

- Not all content formats perform equally well across various social media platforms. Understanding what format best suits your audience is crucial for optimizing engagement.
- **Test Different Formats**: A/B testing can help you determine whether your audience prefers **images**, **videos, carousel posts**, or **text-based updates**. Some audiences engage more with video content, while others may respond better to static visuals or infographics.
- **Example**: Create two versions of the same post—one as a **video** and the other as an **image post**—and compare how each performs in terms of engagement, comments, shares, and overall reach. You can also test carousel posts against single-image posts to see which generates more interaction.

2. **Testing Posting Times**:

  - The timing of your social media posts can significantly impact their **reach** and **engagement**. A/B testing different posting times helps you determine when your audience is most active and responsive.
  - **Experiment with Timing**: Post the same piece of content at **different times of the day** and track engagement levels. For example, test a post at **9 AM** versus **3 PM** on weekdays, or compare weekend post timings to weekday posts.
  - **Data Insights**: By analyzing the data, you can identify patterns and optimize your posting schedule for maximum visibility and interaction. Tools like **Later**, **Buffer**, and **Sprout Social** can help automate posting at the best times based on your findings.

3. Testing Ad Creatives:

For paid social media advertising, A/B testing is essential to improve the performance of your ads. Testing different **ad creatives** helps you determine which elements drive the most conversions and optimize your campaigns.

Elements to Test:

- **Headlines:** Test different headline variations to see which one captures attention more effectively.
- **Images:** Experiment with product images versus lifestyle images or illustrations to see which resonates better with your audience.
- **Call-to-Action (CTA):** A/B test different CTAs, such as "Buy Now" versus "Learn More," to measure which encourages more clicks.
- **Ad Copy:** Test varying lengths or tones of copy. Short, punchy copy might work better for certain products, while longer, more informative text might be ideal for others.

Examples of A/B Testing Experiments to Try

1. Test Different Calls-to-Action (CTAs):

- CTAs are critical in guiding your audience toward a specific action, such as making a purchase, signing up for a newsletter, or visiting your website.

- **Experiment with Variations:** Try variations like "**Shop Now**" vs. "**Learn More**" or "**Get Started**" vs. "**Join the Conversation.**"

- **Track Conversions:** Measure which CTA drives more clicks or conversions. For example, if you're promoting a product, a more urgent CTA like "Shop Now" might lead to higher conversions, while a softer CTA like "Learn More" could be more appropriate for content or brand awareness campaigns.

2. **Test Different Visuals:**

- Visual content plays a significant role in capturing attention on social media. A/B testing different **visual elements** can reveal which ones resonate best with your audience.
- **Visual Experiment**: Test one post with a **product image** and another with a **lifestyle image**. The product image may highlight the features of the item, while the lifestyle image could show the product in use, creating an emotional connection with your audience.
- **Results**: Track which type of visual garners more engagement, such as likes, shares, and comments. It's also useful to assess which visual type works best for different types of posts—promotional, educational, or brand-building.

3. **Test Headline Variations:**

- The headline is often the first thing your audience sees, and a compelling headline can make a significant difference in whether someone engages with your content or not.

- **Headline Experiment**: Try different headline variations for the same content. For example, you could test a **question-based headline** ("Are You Ready to Boost Your Social Media Engagement?") against a **benefit-driven headline** ("Boost Your Social Media Engagement with These Proven Tips").

- **Impact**: This experiment is particularly useful for blog post promotions or longer-form content, as the headline is crucial for attracting attention. Track metrics like click-through rates (CTR) or time spent on the page to determine which headline is more effective at driving traffic and engagement.

Additional A/B Testing Ideas for Social Media

1. **Test Post Length**:

   - For platforms like Twitter or LinkedIn, the length of your post can affect how well it performs. Try **short-form posts** versus **long-form posts** and analyze which ones generate more interaction. For example, test a **concise tweet** against a more detailed post with hashtags or a link to an article.

2. **Test Hashtags**:

   - Hashtags help increase the visibility of your posts, but not all hashtags perform equally well. A/B test using **generic hashtags** versus more **niche-specific ones** to determine which ones lead to more engagement.

   - **Hashtag Experiment**: Test posts with broad hashtags like #SocialMediaMarketing versus more targeted hashtags like #InstagramForBusiness or #ContentCreationTips.

3. **Test Different Platforms**:

   - If your brand is active on multiple social media platforms, you can also A/B test how the same content performs across different platforms. For instance, test the performance of the same post on **Facebook**, **Instagram**, and **LinkedIn** to see which platform drives more engagement for your specific audience.

4. **Test Video Lengths**:

- Video content can be an incredibly engaging format, but the length of the video can impact its performance. A/B test short, **15-30 second videos** against longer **1-2 minute videos** to see which holds attention better and drives more interactions.

Best Practices for A/B Testing

- **Test One Element at a Time**: When performing A/B tests, it's important to test only **one variable** at a time (e.g., changing the CTA or visual) to ensure accurate results. If you test multiple changes at once, you won't know which change caused the outcome.

- **Use Statistical Significance**: To ensure your A/B testing results are reliable, run tests long enough to gather a statistically significant amount of data. This means having enough engagement to confidently say that one version is more effective than the other.

- **Iterate Based on Results**: A/B testing is a continuous process. Once you identify the winning version of a test, use that insight to refine your next round of tests or campaigns.

By regularly incorporating A/B testing into your social media strategy, you can continuously optimize your content, improve your posting strategy, and ensure your paid ads are delivering the best possible results. The ability to test and iterate based on real-time data is one of the most effective ways to stay ahead of the competition and maximize the impact of your social media marketing efforts.

Conclusion

Measuring and analyzing social media performance is crucial for refining your strategy and ensuring your efforts are successful. By understanding key metrics like engagement rate, reach, and conversion rate, and using analytics tools to track performance, you can gain valuable insights that help you optimize your approach. Furthermore, generating meaningful reports allows you to interpret data and refine your strategy, while A/B testing enables you to fine-tune your content and campaigns for maximum impact. By consistently measuring, analyzing, and optimizing, you'll be able to drive better results, foster deeper engagement, and achieve long-term success on social media.

Chapter 7: Leveraging Social Media for Business Growth

Social media has evolved beyond a platform for social interaction into an essential tool for business growth. It offers businesses a unique opportunity to connect with their target audience, drive engagement, and generate leads. In this chapter, we will explore how businesses can leverage social media to accelerate their growth, focusing on lead generation strategies, social selling techniques, and utilizing social media as a customer support channel.

Social Media for Lead Generation

Lead generation is one of the most effective ways businesses can harness the power of social media to drive growth. Social media platforms provide unparalleled access to vast audiences, making them a prime channel for attracting potential customers. When utilized strategically, social media can play a crucial role in capturing high-quality leads. This section delves into proven strategies for using social media to generate leads, including leveraging landing pages, offering lead magnets, running targeted social media ads, and optimizing your profiles for lead conversion.

Strategies for Using Social Media to Capture Leads

Landing Pages:

- **What Are Landing Pages?**

  Landing pages are dedicated, single-focus web pages designed to guide visitors toward a specific action, such as signing up for a newsletter, requesting a demo, downloading a resource, or making a purchase. These pages are integral to lead generation campaigns, particularly when used in conjunction with social media marketing efforts.

- **How to Use Landing Pages on Social Media**:

  Social media can serve as a direct channel to drive traffic to your landing pages, where potential leads can engage with your offers. Here are some ways to utilize landing pages effectively:

- **Linking to Landing Pages**:

  Incorporate links to your landing pages in your social media **bios, posts**, and **stories**. Most platforms allow you to add a link to your bio (Instagram, Twitter, LinkedIn, etc.), which can be a direct access point for users interested in your offers.

- **Strong Calls-to-Action (CTAs)**:

  In your social media content, include compelling CTAs that encourage users to click through to your landing page for more information or to take advantage of special promotions. Phrases like "Learn More," "Sign Up Now," or "Get Your Free Trial" can prompt users to take action.

- **Promoted Posts and Ads:**

Promote your landing pages through social media ads to drive targeted traffic. Craft visually appealing ads with strong messaging to grab attention. Make sure the ad copy clearly communicates the benefit of visiting the landing page, such as exclusive offers or valuable content.

Lead Magnets:

- **What Are Lead Magnets?**

A lead magnet is something valuable offered in exchange for a potential customer's contact information, typically their **email address**. Common lead magnets include **eBooks**, **whitepapers**, **case studies**, **templates**, **checklists**, and **discount codes**.

- **How to Use Lead Magnets on Social Media:**

Social media is an ideal platform to promote your lead magnets to an engaged audience. Here are strategies for maximizing their effectiveness:

- **Share Engaging Content:**

Post content on your social channels that highlights the value of the lead magnet. For example, share snippets or key insights from an **eBook** or **guide** to pique interest, encouraging followers to download the full version in exchange for their contact information.

- **Create Social Media Ads:**

Use targeted ads on platforms like Facebook or LinkedIn to promote your lead magnets, ensuring that the ad copy emphasizes the value of the resource. Focus on the **pain points** your lead magnet solves to entice users.

- **Urgency and Scarcity**: Promote limited-time offers on social media to increase urgency. For example, offer a **free download** that's available only for a limited period or a **discount code** that expires soon to encourage immediate action.

Social Media Ads:

- **The Power of Social Media Ads for Lead Generation**:

Social media ads, especially on platforms like **Facebook**, **Instagram**, **LinkedIn**, and **Twitter**, provide businesses with the ability to create highly targeted campaigns aimed at capturing leads. With sophisticated targeting capabilities, you can reach specific audiences based on **demographics**, **interests**, **behaviors**, and even past interactions with your brand.

Best Practices for Social Media Ads:

- **Compelling Visuals and Copy**: Ensure your ads feature eye-catching visuals and concise, persuasive copy that highlights the benefits of your offer. The message should immediately convey the value and relevance of what you're offering.
- **Effective Calls-to-Action**: Each ad should include a clear **CTA** that directs users to your **lead capture form** or **landing page**. Common CTAs include "Sign Up Today," "Download Now," or "Book a Free Consultation."
- **Retargeting Ads**: Use **remarketing ads** to target users who have already engaged with your brand in some way (e.g., visited your website, interacted with a post, etc.). Retargeting is highly effective in converting leads

who may not have taken action the first time, bringing them back to your landing page or lead magnet with a refreshed offer.

Optimizing Your Profiles for Lead Generation

Profile Optimization:

Your social media profiles act as the first impression potential leads will have of your business. They should be optimized to drive conversions by clearly communicating what your business offers and how people can engage with it. Here's how to optimize your profile for lead generation:

- **Clear Bio and Description**: In your bio or profile description, ensure it is clear who you are, what you offer, and the value you provide. It should leave no confusion for visitors about the next steps they should take to learn more or engage with your brand.

- **Lead-Capture Links**: Include links to landing pages or lead magnets directly in your **bio** or **profile description**. You can also use tools like **Linktree** or **Bio.fm** to display multiple links, directing followers to a variety of lead-generation offers or resources.

Optimizing Your Bio:

- **Clear Call to Action (CTA)**: In your bio, provide a clear CTA such as "Get Your Free Guide" or "Sign Up for a Demo." This directs visitors immediately to the action you want them to take.

- **Contact Information**: Ensure your contact details, such as your **email address** or **phone number**, are easily accessible, especially if you're offering services that require direct communication with your prospects.

- **Landing Page Links**: Include a link to your **landing page** or any active **lead magnet** in your bio. Social platforms like Instagram allow you to link directly in your bio, creating a seamless path for potential leads to follow.

Visual Branding:

- **Consistency and Trust**: Consistent and professional visual branding builds trust and helps establish credibility with your potential leads. Use high-quality imagery, clear branding elements, and cohesive **color schemes** across your social media profiles.

- **Promote Lead-Generating Offers**: Your **profile banners** or **headers** should highlight any current **lead generation campaigns** or **special offers**. For example, if you are promoting a limited-time eBook download, feature the offer in your cover photo along with a CTA like "Download Now."

Instagram Stories and Highlights:

- Instagram **Stories** and **Highlights** provide excellent opportunities to promote your lead generation efforts. Use Stories to showcase your **lead magnets**, promote **limited-time offers**, or direct users to your **landing pages**. Pin these Stories as **Highlights** on your profile for easy access by visitors.

By effectively combining landing pages, lead magnets, social media ads, and profile optimization, businesses can significantly enhance their lead generation efforts on social media. Social media platforms offer a unique opportunity to engage directly with potential customers, making it essential to implement strategies that drive both awareness and conversions. With these tactics in place, you can build a steady stream of qualified leads and fuel long-term business growth.

Social Selling Techniques

Social selling is the practice of leveraging social media platforms to build relationships with potential clients and customers, position your brand as a trusted resource, and create opportunities for conversions and long-term customer loyalty. Whether you're focused on B2B (business-to-business) or B2C (business-to-consumer) sales, mastering social selling can be a game-changer for establishing meaningful connections and driving business growth.

Using LinkedIn for B2B Sales

LinkedIn Profile Optimization for Social Selling:

LinkedIn is one of the most powerful tools for B2B sales, offering businesses the ability to engage with other companies and build professional relationships. To maximize its potential, your LinkedIn profile should be strategically optimized to make a great first impression and build credibility.

- **Profile Picture & Headline:** Ensure your profile features a professional and approachable photo. The headline should clearly communicate what you do and how you help businesses solve problems.

- **Detailed Summary:** The "About" section should outline your expertise, experience, and the specific solutions your business offers. Be clear about the value you can bring to potential clients.

- **Social Proof:** Adding client testimonials, case studies, and project highlights is essential to provide credibility and build trust. Recommendations and endorsements from colleagues or clients can be a powerful form of social proof.

- **Clear Call-to-Action (CTA):** Add a CTA in your profile that encourages potential clients to contact you for consultations, demos, or further discussion on services.

Building Relationships Through Content:

LinkedIn thrives on valuable, thought-provoking content. Sharing industry insights, case studies, whitepapers, or blog posts not only educates your audience but positions you as a trusted thought leader in your field.

- **Post Regularly:** Share content that speaks to the pain points of your target audience and aligns with their business needs. Posting regularly keeps you top of mind.

- **Engagement:** Actively engage with content posted by others. Like, comment, and share posts from potential clients and industry influencers. By engaging in meaningful conversations, you increase your visibility and credibility.

- **LinkedIn Articles:** Publishing long-form articles on LinkedIn can further establish you as an expert in your field. It's an opportunity to showcase deep knowledge on specific industry trends and challenges.

Personalized Outreach:

Avoid generic, mass connection requests. Personalized outreach is key to social selling on LinkedIn. Here's how to approach it:

- **Tailor Connection Requests:** When sending a connection request, customize your message to explain why connecting could be mutually beneficial. Reference mutual connections, shared interests, or specific reasons for reaching out.

- **Value-Driven Messaging:** Once connected, don't immediately go into a sales pitch. Instead, focus on building rapport by offering helpful resources, articles, or insights related to their industry.

- **Follow-Up:** If they engage with your content, follow up with a message expressing appreciation and suggesting further conversations or solutions. Avoid being overly aggressive; instead, focus on being helpful and building trust over time.

Using Facebook for B2C Interactions

1. Targeting the Right Audience with Facebook Ads:

Facebook is one of the most popular social platforms for B2C businesses, offering sophisticated targeting options to help you reach the exact audience that is most likely to convert into paying customers.

- **Refined Targeting:** Use Facebook's ad targeting tools to segment your audience by age, location, interests, and behaviors. For example, if you sell fitness products, target individuals who show an interest in health, wellness, or fitness-related activities.

- **Lead Generation Ads:** Facebook offers specific ad formats for capturing leads directly on the platform. These ads allow users to submit their contact information (like email or phone number) without leaving Facebook, making it a seamless experience.

- **Compelling Ad Copy and Visuals:** Your ad copy should highlight the benefits of your product or service, accompanied by eye-catching visuals. Use high-quality images or videos that align with your brand's aesthetic and grab the user's attention.

- **Limited-Time Offers:** Consider using limited-time promotions or exclusive offers to create urgency and encourage immediate action. These time-sensitive offers can help push prospects into making a decision.

2. **Engaging with Consumers Through Facebook Groups:**

Facebook Groups are an excellent platform for building a community around your brand and engaging directly with your target audience.

- **Create a Niche Group:** Develop a group centered around a specific interest or industry that your product or service aligns with. For example, if you're selling eco-friendly products, create a group focused on sustainability or green living.

- **Active Participation:** Regularly participate in discussions, offer expert insights, and answer questions. By offering value to group members, you establish credibility and build trust.

- **Content Sharing:** Share blog posts, articles, and resources in the group that address common pain points or provide value to the members. This positions your brand as a helpful resource and can lead to conversions over time.

- **Encourage Engagement:** Foster active discussions among group members by asking questions, running polls, or encouraging feedback. The more engagement you generate, the more likely it is that group members will trust you and convert into customers.

3. **Relationship Building Through Direct Messages:**

Facebook Messenger is one of the most personal forms of communication on social media. It's an excellent tool for connecting directly with potential customers and nurturing relationships.

- **Initial Conversations:** After a user interacts with your content or engages with your brand in a group, send a friendly and personalized message. Offer assistance or advice based on their interests or needs. The key is to focus on the relationship rather than making an immediate sale.

- **Provide Value:** In your messages, share helpful information, tips, or resources that are relevant to the individual. Whether it's a product recommendation, a how-to guide, or a discount code, ensure that what you offer is aligned with their interests.

- **Avoid Being Pushy:** Social selling is about building trust over time. Don't rush into selling your products or services. Instead, focus on building rapport and ensuring that your products meet their needs. If the person isn't ready to buy yet, continue nurturing the relationship until they are.

4. **Using Facebook Messenger Bots for Automation:**

For businesses that receive a high volume of inquiries, automating some aspects of communication can be incredibly beneficial. Facebook Messenger bots can help by responding to initial inquiries, providing information, or scheduling appointments automatically.

- **Automated Greetings:** Set up a bot that sends a friendly greeting as soon as someone messages your business page. You can use this to gather basic information or direct users to a relevant part of your website.

- **Lead Capture:** Bots can ask qualifying questions and capture lead information (such as email addresses or product preferences) before handing the conversation off to a human representative.

- **24/7 Availability:** Bots can assist customers at any time of day, helping you engage with prospects even outside of business hours. This increases your chances of generating leads and improving customer satisfaction.

Social selling on platforms like LinkedIn and Facebook involves more than just selling; it's about building genuine relationships, offering value, and becoming a trusted resource in your industry. By optimizing your profiles, sharing valuable content, and engaging in personalized outreach, you can leverage these platforms to not only generate leads but also cultivate long-term, loyal customers.

Customer Support and Service

Social media has evolved from a tool for brand promotion to an essential channel for customer support and service. Customers expect real-time responses and personalized assistance through these platforms. Providing excellent customer service on social media not only resolves issues but also helps foster strong relationships, builds brand loyalty, and enhances the overall customer experience.

How to Use Social Media as a Customer Support Channel

Quick Response Times:

One of the most significant advantages of social media for customer support is its immediacy. Customers often expect faster response times on social media than through traditional channels like email or phone.

- **Real-Time Monitoring:** Establish a strategy to monitor your social media platforms for any customer inquiries or comments, ensuring that you're always aware of customer needs. Use social media management tools to keep track of messages, mentions, and direct inquiries across various channels.

- **Dedicated Support Team:** Assign a team member or create a dedicated social media support team responsible for responding to customer inquiries. The quicker you can respond, the more likely customers are to feel valued and satisfied with your service.

- **Set Expectations:** Make sure to communicate your expected response time on your social media pages so customers understand when they can expect a reply. If real-time responses aren't possible, acknowledge the message and inform the customer when they can expect a detailed response.

Public and Private Responses:

When dealing with customer inquiries, there's a balance between addressing issues publicly and privately. The way you respond can influence the customer's perception of your brand, so it's essential to manage both approaches effectively.

- **Public Acknowledgment:** Publicly acknowledge customer issues to demonstrate that you're attentive and care about their concerns. A brief response like, "Thank you for your feedback! We're sorry to hear about your experience and will resolve this as quickly as possible" can go a long way in showing your willingness to help.

- **Take Conversations Private:** Once you've acknowledged the complaint publicly, it's often best to move the conversation to a private channel, like Direct Messages or Messenger. This allows for a more in-depth, personalized response while keeping sensitive information confidential.

- **Transparency and Privacy:** Acknowledge the issue publicly and demonstrate transparency, but resolve the issue privately to protect customer information and maintain professionalism. This ensures that all inquiries are handled appropriately without escalating the situation in a public forum.

Handling Negative Feedback and Resolving Customer Complaints

1. Stay Calm and Professional:

Negative feedback is an inevitable part of business, but how you handle it can significantly impact your reputation. Always remain calm and professional, even in the face of challenging or critical feedback.

- **Acknowledge the Issue:** Start by acknowledging the customer's frustration and expressing empathy. Use phrases like, "We're really sorry that you had a negative experience, and we appreciate you bringing this to our attention."

- **Avoid Defensiveness:** Resist the urge to become defensive or argumentative. Customers are more likely to feel heard and valued if you maintain a calm demeanor and focus on finding solutions rather than justifying your actions.

- **Solution-Oriented:** After empathizing with the customer, work towards offering a solution. Let them know that you're committed to resolving the issue and improving their experience. Be clear about next steps and timeframes.

2. Address Issues Promptly:

Delays in addressing complaints can significantly damage your brand's reputation. Promptly responding and resolving issues helps to demonstrate that you prioritize customer satisfaction.

- **Speed of Response:** The quicker you respond, the more likely customers are to view your brand favorably, even if the initial experience was negative. If resolving the issue takes time, keep the customer updated on progress.

- **Resolution and Follow-Up:** Once the issue has been resolved, thank the customer for their patience and ask if they are satisfied with the solution. If applicable, politely ask if they would be willing to amend their public feedback or share a positive update to reflect the resolution.

- **Continuous Improvement:** Use feedback as an opportunity for growth. If you see recurring complaints about a specific issue, take steps to address the root cause and prevent future occurrences.

Turning Satisfied Customers into Brand Advocates

1. **Encourage Positive Reviews and Testimonials:**

One of the most effective ways to build social proof and trust is through customer reviews and testimonials. Satisfied customers are often willing to share their positive experiences, which can influence potential buyers.

- **Request Reviews:** After successfully resolving an issue or providing excellent service, ask customers if they'd be willing to leave a review on your social media pages or third-party review platforms. Make it easy by providing direct links to your review pages.

- **Incentivize Feedback:** Consider offering incentives, such as discounts, exclusive offers, or entry into a prize draw, to encourage customers to share their feedback. This can motivate customers to leave detailed reviews that reflect their satisfaction.

- **Highlight Positive Feedback:** Share positive reviews and testimonials on your social media profiles, website, and other marketing materials. This reinforces your brand's reputation for quality service.

2. User-Generated Content (UGC):

User-generated content is one of the most powerful forms of social proof, as it showcases real people using and enjoying your products or services. UGC can significantly boost brand visibility and engagement.

- **Encourage Sharing:** Ask customers to share photos, videos, or stories of themselves using your products or services. You can incentivize them by offering rewards or featuring their content in your social media campaigns.

- **Repost and Share:** When customers tag your brand or share their experiences, repost their content on your social media pages. This not only strengthens customer relationships but also showcases real-life endorsements.

- **Special Features:** Spotlight loyal customers by featuring them as part of a "Customer of the Month" series or similar initiatives. Publicly recognizing their loyalty and support can increase engagement and encourage others to participate.

3. **Building a Community of Advocates:**

A strong and engaged community is one of the best ways to ensure long-term customer loyalty. By fostering an environment where your customers feel valued and heard, you can cultivate a network of brand advocates.

- **Create Exclusive Communities:** Develop a private Facebook Group or other community spaces where satisfied customers can connect with your brand, ask questions, and share feedback. This builds a sense of belonging and encourages ongoing engagement.

- **Host Special Events:** Offer early access to new products, exclusive events, or special promotions for your brand advocates. This creates a sense of exclusivity that makes customers feel valued and appreciated.

- **Referral Programs:** Create a referral program that rewards existing customers for recommending your products or services to others. This incentivizes satisfied customers to spread the word about your brand, turning them into active promoters.

By developing strong, loyal relationships with your customers, you can not only improve retention rates but also turn your satisfied customers into powerful advocates who will help grow your brand organically.

Conclusion

Social media is an invaluable tool for customer support and service. By providing quick responses, handling complaints professionally, and transforming satisfied customers into brand advocates, you can use social media not only to resolve issues but to build stronger, more meaningful relationships with your customers. Social media, when leveraged correctly, can serve as a pivotal tool for fostering brand loyalty, improving customer retention, and driving business growth.

Leveraging social media for business growth is a dynamic, multifaceted strategy that involves more than just posting content. From generating leads and using social selling techniques to offering top-notch customer service, social media offers a wealth of opportunities for businesses to thrive. By utilizing these strategies effectively, businesses can strengthen their online presence, build stronger relationships with prospects and customers, and ultimately drive long-term growth. The key lies in providing value, engaging with your audience authentically, and using social media to create lasting connections that benefit both your business and your customers.

Chapter 8: Advanced Social Media Tactics

As businesses look to stay competitive in a fast-moving digital landscape, mastering advanced social media tactics becomes increasingly important. The ability to use social media effectively not only enhances engagement and drives brand awareness but also enables businesses to streamline operations and reach new audiences. In this chapter, we will explore some advanced social media strategies that can take your business's social media presence to the next level. Topics covered will include social media automation, harnessing user-generated content, and leveraging social media trends.

Utilizing Social Media Automation

Social media automation has become a powerful tool for businesses looking to streamline their social media activities and maximize their online presence. It involves using software tools to manage tasks such as scheduling posts, responding to comments, and sending direct messages. Automation can help businesses save valuable time and effort, allowing teams to focus on other critical functions. However, it's essential to use automation strategically to ensure that the human touch—vital for building relationships—is not lost in the process. In this section, we explore the tools, strategies, benefits, and potential risks associated with automating social media efforts.

Tools and Strategies for Automating Social Media Posts and Responses

1. Social Media Scheduling Tools

Scheduling tools are among the most widely used automation tools for managing social media activities. These tools allow businesses to plan and automate their posts across multiple social platforms, maintaining consistency and saving time. The use of scheduling tools ensures that posts go live at optimal times without requiring manual intervention. Here are some popular scheduling tools:

- **Hootsuite:** A robust social media management tool that supports multiple social networks like Facebook, Twitter, Instagram, and LinkedIn. Hootsuite allows businesses to schedule posts, monitor social media conversations, and measure the performance of campaigns.

- **Buffer:** Buffer is another widely used platform for scheduling posts, tracking content performance, and collaborating with team members. It provides insights and analytics to track engagement and improve future posts.

- **Sprout Social:** A comprehensive social media platform that not only handles post scheduling but also provides tools for engagement, reporting, and customer service. It enables businesses to manage multiple social accounts from a single dashboard.

Best Practices for Scheduling Posts:

- **Plan in advance**: Strategically plan content to align with marketing campaigns or seasonal trends. Schedule posts to align with times when your target audience is most active.

- **Use evergreen content**: Content that doesn't go out of date can be reused periodically. Evergreen posts can help maintain activity on your social profiles even when new content is not being created daily.

- **Monitor and refine**: Regularly check the performance of automated posts to ensure they remain relevant and accurate. Automation should complement but not replace human oversight.

2. Automated Responses

Automating responses to common inquiries or frequently asked questions (FAQs) can significantly improve efficiency, especially in handling a high volume of inquiries. Automation tools such as chatbots and instant reply features on social platforms can provide immediate assistance to customers.

- **ManyChat:** This tool specializes in automating interactions on Facebook Messenger. Businesses can set up workflows to respond to inquiries based on keywords or customer actions (e.g., providing product details or assisting with orders).

- **MobileMonkey:** A platform for automating customer interactions on Facebook Messenger, Instagram, and SMS. It allows businesses to engage customers with tailored automated responses and even segment users based on their interactions.

- **Intercom:** This tool enables businesses to automate customer service across multiple channels, including chat, email, and in-app messaging. Intercom's automation also helps segment customers for personalized interactions.

Best Practices for Automating Responses:

- **Keep it simple and helpful:** Automated responses should be brief, clear, and to the point. Avoid overly complex or robotic language, as it may frustrate users.

- **Escalate when necessary:** Automation should not replace human interaction entirely. Ensure that complex or personalized inquiries are transferred to a live representative as needed.

- **Test responses:** Regularly test and tweak automated responses to ensure they meet customer needs and expectations effectively.

Pros and Cons of Social Media Automation

Pros:

1. **Time Efficiency:** Automation reduces the time spent on repetitive tasks such as posting content and responding to routine inquiries. This allows your team to focus on higher-level strategy, creativity, and relationship building.

2. **Consistency**: Social media automation ensures that your social profiles remain active and consistently updated, even during off-hours or when your team is unavailable. This is particularly beneficial for businesses with a global audience or those operating in multiple time zones.

3. **Better Analytics**: Many social media automation tools provide detailed analytics that help businesses track the performance of their posts, identify successful content, and refine their strategies for future campaigns.

Cons:

1. **Loss of Personal Touch**: While automation offers efficiency, over-reliance on it can make interactions feel impersonal. Social media is a platform built for engagement and relationship-building, and relying solely on automated content and responses can undermine your brand's human touch.

2. **Potential Mistakes**: Despite their capabilities, automation tools can sometimes make errors, such as scheduling irrelevant posts, sending incorrect messages, or failing to adapt to a fast-changing social media landscape. These mistakes can harm a brand's reputation if not properly managed.

3. **Missed Opportunities for Real-time Engagement**: Automated tools may cause businesses to miss out on opportunities for real-time engagement with current trends, customer feedback, or viral topics. Social media is highly dynamic, and some situations require a spontaneous, human response.

Striking the Right Balance with Automation

While automation can bring significant advantages, businesses must strike a balance between efficiency and personalization. Social media thrives on real-time interaction and human connections, which are crucial for building lasting relationships with customers. The key to successful social media automation lies in ensuring that automated tools complement, rather than replace, the personal engagement that social platforms are known for. By strategically leveraging automation for time-consuming tasks, businesses can free up resources for more valuable, high-touch interactions, enhancing their social media presence and customer satisfaction.

Harnessing User-Generated Content

User-generated content (UGC) is any content created by customers or followers that features a brand, product, or service, rather than the brand creating it themselves. This content can take many forms, including photos, videos, reviews, testimonials, or social media posts. UGC is incredibly valuable for businesses because it provides social proof, boosts brand authenticity, and engages customers in a more personal way. In this section, we'll explore how businesses can encourage users to create content and run successful hashtag campaigns to amplify their brand.

Encouraging Followers to Create Content for Your Brand

1. Create Shareable Content

The foundation of successful UGC lies in producing content that your audience wants to engage with and share. By focusing on making your content visually appealing, informative, and relatable to your target demographic, you set the stage for customers to share your brand with their own networks.

- **Appealing Visuals**: High-quality, eye-catching images and videos are more likely to be shared. People love content that is aesthetically pleasing or provides visual storytelling that resonates with them.

- **Incorporate Your Brand's Personality**: Whether your brand voice is humorous, inspirational, or educational, it should be present in all content. Emotional triggers play a big role in content virality— when users feel something, they're more likely to share. Align the content with your brand's personality to strengthen that connection with followers.

- **Relatability**: Ensure that your content speaks directly to the interests, values, and lifestyle of your audience. The more relatable your content is, the more likely followers will want to engage with it, share it, and even create their own content inspired by it.

2. Host Contests and Giveaways

Running social media contests or giveaways is one of the most effective ways to encourage UGC. Offering an incentive such as a prize or special recognition provides motivation for users to create and share content that involves your brand.

- **How It Works**: For example, ask your followers to submit photos or videos using your product in creative ways, or encourage them to share a story about how your service has helped them. In exchange, they could win something valuable like a free product, a gift card, or a feature on your brand's social media page.

- **Clear Instructions**: Be sure to set clear, easy-to-follow guidelines for entering the contest. Specify what content you're looking for (e.g., photos, videos, stories) and how to submit it. This helps ensure that you receive high-quality, relevant content.

- **Engagement**: Contests also foster engagement with your community, allowing them to interact directly with your brand in a fun and meaningful way. As participants submit content, it creates excitement and buzz around your brand.

3. Repost User Content

When followers create content featuring your brand, reposting it on your own social media channels is a great way to show appreciation, build community, and encourage others to create content.

- **Give Credit**: Always ask for permission to repost user-generated content, and be sure to credit the original creator by tagging them in your post. This not only acknowledges their effort but also fosters goodwill.

- **Incentivize Sharing**: Users are more likely to create content if they know there's a chance it could be featured. This also increases the visibility of your brand, as users with a large following might share the reposted content, extending your reach.

- **Build a Sense of Community**: Reposting user content highlights how your brand resonates with real people, further reinforcing the community aspect of your brand. This increases authenticity and helps build stronger emotional connections with your audience.

How to Run Successful Hashtag Campaigns

Hashtags are one of the most effective tools for organizing and promoting user-generated content. By creating a campaign-specific hashtag, you encourage your followers to share their content, which in turn boosts your visibility and helps you track engagement around a particular theme or event.

1. Choose a Memorable and Relevant Hashtag

A well-crafted hashtag is essential for the success of your UGC campaign. It should be easy to remember, simple to spell, and align with your brand's messaging.

- **Catchy and Easy-to-Spell**: Choose a hashtag that sticks in people's minds and is simple to type. If the hashtag is too complicated or long, users may not remember it, limiting participation.

- **Reflect Your Brand and Campaign Theme**: Ensure the hashtag captures the essence of your campaign. A strong hashtag should be directly linked to your brand's identity and the message you want to convey. For example, Coca-Cola's #ShareACoke campaign was effective because it tapped into the personal and social nature of sharing a Coke with friends, making it easy for users to relate to and participate.

- **Encourage Creativity**: A great hashtag should also be flexible enough to allow creativity from users. You want followers to feel like they can put their unique spin on it, which increases the likelihood of user participation.

2. Promote the Hashtag Across Multiple Channels

Once you've created your campaign hashtag, it's time to spread the word. Promote the hashtag across all your social media channels and encourage followers to use it when sharing content related to your brand or campaign.

- **Cross-Channel Promotion**: Don't limit the campaign to just one platform. Promote your hashtag on Instagram, Facebook, Twitter, LinkedIn, and even on your website. The more places your audience sees it, the more likely they are to engage.

- **Incentives to Participate**: Give followers a reason to use the hashtag. Offer incentives such as the chance to win a prize, be featured on your page, or gain recognition from your brand. This can increase engagement and excitement around the campaign.

- **Clear Calls to Action**: Encourage your followers with a clear call to action, such as "Share your experience with [Brand Name] using #YourBrandStory for a chance to win a free product!" This simple request will guide them to take action.

3. Monitor Hashtag Engagement

To make the most of your hashtag campaign, you need to monitor how it's performing and engage with those participating.

- **Track Hashtag Usage**: Use social media monitoring tools like **Hootsuite** or **Sprout Social** to track the use of your hashtag. These tools provide insights into how many times the hashtag has been used, the level of engagement it has received, and where it's gaining the most traction.

- **Engage with Users**: Actively engage with users who are using your hashtag. Respond to their posts, share some of the best user-generated content, and even continue the conversation. This helps build momentum and keeps the campaign alive.

- **Measure Success**: Analyze the success of your campaign by evaluating key metrics such as the number of hashtag uses, user engagement, and overall brand reach. Adjust your strategy based on these insights to improve future hashtag campaigns.

Conclusion

Harnessing user-generated content (UGC) through campaigns, contests, and hashtags is a powerful way to build brand credibility, engage with your audience, and increase brand visibility. By creating shareable, relatable content, encouraging participation, and running targeted hashtag campaigns, you can significantly amplify your brand's reach and authenticity. However, remember that UGC should be nurtured and celebrated to maintain a positive and engaging relationship with your customers.

Leveraging Social Media Trends

Social media trends present a valuable opportunity for businesses to stay relevant, engage with a broader audience, and increase visibility in an ever-changing digital landscape. Trends can take various forms, including viral challenges, new content formats like Reels or TikTok videos, and trending hashtags. By staying attuned to these developments, businesses can leverage them to enhance their social media presence and connect with followers in creative ways.

Staying Up-to-Date with the Latest Trends

1. Follow Trendsetters

- To effectively tap into social media trends, it's crucial to monitor the right influencers and accounts that lead the charge in setting trends.

- **Industry Influencers and Thought Leaders**: Follow key figures within your industry who often kickstart or highlight emerging trends. These accounts are excellent sources for discovering fresh content ideas or viral movements.

- **Popular Social Media Accounts**: Platforms like Instagram, Twitter, TikTok, and YouTube are home to accounts with substantial followings that are known for driving trends. Keep an eye on their posts and activities to stay ahead of the curve. These accounts often experiment with content types that resonate with their audiences and quickly gain momentum.

- **Trend Prediction Accounts**: Some accounts and platforms are specifically dedicated to forecasting or curating trends across various industries. Subscribing to these can provide you with a competitive edge in spotting what's coming next.

2. Use Trend Analysis Tools

- Utilizing trend analysis tools is essential to identify the topics, themes, and content formats that are gaining traction.

- **Google Trends**: This free tool helps you track the popularity of search terms over time and spot rising trends in various categories. By exploring what's trending globally or regionally, you can adjust your content strategy to match the zeitgeist.

- **Twitter Trending Topics**: Twitter's trending section is a real-time showcase of what's being discussed across the globe. By keeping track of these conversations, you can discover new movements, topics, or hashtags that are relevant to your brand.

- **Social Listening Tools**: Platforms like Hootsuite, Sprout Social, and BuzzSumo help monitor trends and conversations in your niche. These tools allow you to identify what's resonating with your audience and spot opportunities for real-time engagement.

3. Engage with Viral Content

- One of the most impactful ways to leverage trends is by actively participating in viral content or trending topics. This helps increase your brand's reach and allows you to join relevant conversations in real time.

- **Jump on Viral Challenges**: TikTok, Instagram, and Twitter are home to viral challenges that businesses can participate in. Whether it's a fun hashtag, dance challenge, or meme, joining these movements can dramatically amplify your brand's visibility. Be sure that the challenge is relevant to your brand identity and message.

- **Use Trending Hashtags**: Take advantage of trending hashtags that are relevant to your business or industry. These hashtags help you appear in trending discussions and boost your discoverability on platforms like Twitter, Instagram, and LinkedIn. When you post with these hashtags, your content reaches a broader audience beyond your current followers.

- **Be Timely and Relatable**: Engaging with viral content requires quick thinking and fast execution. When trends emerge, act quickly—timeliness is key to capturing the moment before the trend fades. Also, ensure your content is relatable to your audience to maximize engagement.

Incorporating Trends into Your Social Media Strategy

1. Adapt Trends to Fit Your Brand Voice

- While it's tempting to jump on every trend that pops up, it's essential to remain true to your brand voice and values. Inauthentic participation can backfire and harm your brand's credibility.

- **Stay Authentic**: Trends should align with your brand's identity. If your brand is known for its serious tone, for example, it might not be appropriate to jump on a lighthearted meme or dance challenge. Consider if the trend fits your image or if it will make your brand seem forced or out of place.

- **Maintain Consistency**: When adapting trends, ensure they support your overall social media strategy and messaging. If a trend is too disconnected from your brand's core values, it's better to pass on it and wait for one that feels more aligned.

- **Relatable Content**: Even if you're participating in a trend, always make sure your content speaks to your audience's interests or needs. Whether it's humor, inspiration, or education, tailoring trends to fit your brand will ensure they resonate with your community.

2. Experiment with New Formats

- Social media platforms regularly introduce new features, and experimenting with these can help you stay at the forefront of engagement.

- **Short-Form Video Content**: Embrace formats like Instagram Reels, TikTok videos, or YouTube Shorts to engage with a younger, more dynamic audience. These formats are highly engaging and offer ample opportunities to showcase creativity, from behind-the-scenes footage to product demos and customer highlights.

- **Interactive Stories and Polls**: Instagram Stories, Facebook Stories, and other interactive features (like polls, quizzes, and questions) allow for more direct engagement with followers. They are especially effective for fostering two-way communication and gaining feedback from your audience.

- **Trending Music and Challenges**: Incorporating trending music, themes, or viral challenges into your video content is a great way to increase visibility and engagement. Leverage these formats to create entertaining and shareable content that fits the trend while still being true to your brand.

3. Create Your Own Trend

- While following trends is important, creating your own trend is an excellent way to establish your brand as a thought leader and trendsetter in your industry.

- **Branded Challenges**: Start a challenge that encourages user participation and interaction. For example, a fashion brand might launch a #MyStyleMyWay challenge, encouraging followers to share their unique outfits. A fitness brand could create a challenge around a particular exercise routine.

- **Hashtag Campaigns**: Create a campaign-specific hashtag that encourages users to engage with your brand. A hashtag like #CleanBeautyRevolution could inspire followers to share their favorite clean beauty products, positioning your brand as a leader in the movement.

- **Viral Content Creation**: In addition to hashtags and challenges, consider creating viral content that's designed to capture attention. Whether it's a humorous video, a heartwarming customer story, or a surprising product reveal, aim to create content that can easily be shared and spread across social platforms.

Conclusion

Leveraging social media trends can significantly boost your brand's visibility and engagement. By staying updated with the latest trends, engaging with viral content, and incorporating them into your social media strategy, you can amplify your brand's voice and connect with a wider audience. However, it's important to balance staying on trend with maintaining authenticity. Whether you're adapting existing trends or creating your own, being mindful of your brand's voice will help ensure your participation remains genuine and valuable.

Advanced social media tactics, such as automation, leveraging user-generated content, and staying on top of trends, can provide significant advantages for businesses looking to deepen engagement, expand their reach, and streamline operations. By using these strategies effectively, businesses can not only optimize their social media efforts but also create a more authentic, interactive experience for their audience. Social media is an ever-evolving landscape, and staying ahead of the curve with these advanced tactics will give your brand the edge it needs to thrive in today's digital world.

Chapter 9: Social Media Do's and Don'ts

Social media has become an essential tool for businesses to engage with their audience, promote products or services, and build brand awareness. However, navigating the world of social media can be tricky. While it offers a vast array of opportunities, it also comes with potential pitfalls. In this chapter, we will explore the common mistakes to avoid, the essential etiquette for social media interactions, and how to manage a crisis when negative publicity arises.

Common Mistakes to Avoid

To succeed on social media, businesses must navigate the complexities of engagement, content strategy, and brand identity carefully. Certain mistakes, if not addressed, can derail growth and engagement. In this section, we will explore some of the most common errors businesses make on social media and provide actionable strategies to avoid them.

1. Overposting or Underposting

Finding the right posting frequency can be challenging. Both overposting and underposting can negatively affect your brand's visibility and engagement on social media.

Overposting

While consistency is key to building an online presence, flooding your followers' feeds with too many posts can overwhelm them, leading to disengagement. Overposting often occurs when a business tries to maximize its exposure by posting excessively, but this strategy can backfire if it becomes repetitive or feels too much like a hard sell.

- **Why It's a Mistake**: Overposting can annoy followers, leading them to unfollow or mute your account. If your audience feels like they are constantly being marketed to, they may disengage altogether.

- **How to Avoid Overposting**:

    o **Stick to a Content Calendar**: Develop a content schedule to help you maintain regularity without bombarding your audience. Platforms have different optimal posting frequencies; for example, Instagram users may appreciate 1-2 posts per day, while Twitter users often expect more frequent posts (3-5 tweets a day).

    o **Monitor Engagement**: Track your engagement metrics and adjust your posting frequency based on audience reactions. If you notice a drop in likes, comments, or shares after a certain frequency, it might be time to scale back. Using social media analytics tools can help you understand when your audience is most responsive.

Underposting

On the other hand, underposting—posting too infrequently—can make your business appear inactive or disconnected from its audience. Social media platforms prioritize active accounts that provide regular content, so infrequent posting can diminish your chances of being discovered or staying top of mind.

- **Why It's a Mistake**: Underposting can cause your brand to fade into obscurity. If followers don't see fresh content regularly, they may forget about your business, or worse, perceive your brand as stagnant.

- **How to Avoid Underposting**:

    o **Diversify Your Content**: Develop a content strategy that includes a mix of content types such as promotions, educational posts, behind-the-scenes looks, user-generated content, and interactive posts. A variety of content keeps your audience engaged without overwhelming them.

    o **Use Scheduling Tools**: Tools like Hootsuite, Buffer, and Sprout Social can help you schedule posts in advance, ensuring consistent activity on your social media accounts even if you can't post in real-time every day. These tools also let you plan content ahead of time, so your posts are well thought out and strategically timed.

2. Ignoring Comments and Engagement

Social media is not just a platform for broadcasting your message—it's about building relationships with your audience. Ignoring comments, direct messages, and mentions is a critical mistake many businesses make, whether due to limited resources or prioritization issues. Engagement is a two-way street, and failing to respond can erode customer trust and loyalty.

- **Why It's a Mistake**: Ignoring engagement can lead to missed opportunities to build relationships, address concerns, or even gain customer insights. It also makes your business seem unapproachable or uninterested in customer feedback.

- **How to Avoid Ignoring Engagement**:

    - **Set Aside Dedicated Time for Engagement**: Make social media interaction a priority by designating time daily or weekly to respond to comments, messages, and mentions. Engaging with your followers shows that you care about their opinions and helps foster a sense of community.

    - **Respond to All Feedback**: Acknowledge both positive and negative comments in a timely and respectful manner. Addressing complaints publicly can showcase your commitment to customer service and your willingness to resolve issues. For example, if someone complains about a product, a timely, empathetic response can demonstrate your dedication to customer satisfaction.

- o **Create a Community**: Engage in ongoing conversations with your audience. Ask for their opinions, encourage them to share their thoughts, and respond to comments to foster a loyal online community. Customers are more likely to continue engaging with a brand that interacts with them.

3. Inconsistent Branding

Your social media presence should reflect the same consistency as your overall brand identity. This includes visual elements (logos, color schemes, fonts), tone of voice, and messaging. Inconsistent branding can confuse followers, make your posts seem disjointed, and ultimately diminish your credibility.

- **Why It's a Mistake**: Inconsistent branding dilutes your brand identity, leaving your audience unsure about what your business stands for. It also creates a fragmented customer experience across platforms, making it harder for followers to connect with your brand.

- **How to Avoid Inconsistent Branding**:

  - o **Develop a Comprehensive Brand Guide**: Create a brand guide that outlines your visual elements, tone of voice, messaging, and content style. This ensures everyone managing your social media accounts is aligned and presents a cohesive brand image. The guide should cover specifics such as the types of language and tone you use (e.g., friendly, professional, humorous) and visual guidelines (e.g., logos, color palette, font choices).

- **Ensure Brand Alignment Across All Channels:** Every post should reflect your brand's mission and values, whether you're sharing an educational blog, a promotional offer, or a behind-the-scenes glimpse. Avoid jumping on trends or using content that doesn't align with your values just for the sake of engagement. For example, if your brand is known for eco-consciousness, don't promote a non-sustainable product even if it's trending at the moment.

- **Review Your Content Regularly:** Conduct regular audits of your social media accounts to ensure that all posts and visuals are consistent with your brand guidelines. Over time, trends, audience preferences, and content formats may change, but your brand's core identity should remain intact.

Conclusion

Avoiding common social media mistakes can significantly improve your brand's engagement, visibility, and overall success online. By finding the right balance between posting frequency, actively engaging with your followers, and maintaining consistent branding, you can avoid pitfalls that may hinder growth. Social media is a dynamic and interactive space, and businesses that embrace best practices and stay authentic to their brand will build stronger connections with their audience and achieve long-term success.

Social Media Etiquette

In addition to avoiding common mistakes, businesses must be mindful of the unspoken rules and best practices that govern social media interactions. Proper etiquette ensures that a brand maintains professionalism, builds trust with its audience, and cultivates goodwill. While the specific etiquette for each platform can vary, there are several general principles that apply across the board. By adhering to these rules, businesses can establish a positive and authentic social media presence.

1. Understanding the Unspoken Rules of Each Platform

Each social media platform has a unique culture and set of unwritten rules that shape how users engage with content. Understanding these platform-specific nuances helps businesses communicate more effectively and develop stronger relationships with their followers.

Instagram

Instagram thrives on visual storytelling. High-quality images and videos that reflect your brand's visual identity perform best. The platform encourages a casual, authentic approach to content through features like Stories, Reels, and carousel posts. Influencer marketing is also highly impactful on Instagram, where users are accustomed to seeing collaborations between brands and influencers.

> **Etiquette Tip**: Avoid overloading your feed with promotional content. Focus instead on storytelling, sharing behind-the-scenes glimpses of your business, and showcasing user-generated content. Engage with your followers by responding to comments and direct messages (DMs) to foster a sense of community.

Facebook

Facebook is a blend of personal and professional connections, making it a unique platform for businesses. While Facebook is often used for promotional content, it is also a space where users engage in discussions and share personal updates. The key to success on Facebook is creating meaningful interactions and being part of conversations.

> **Etiquette Tip**: Don't bombard your followers with constant sales pitches. Instead, focus on building a community by sharing valuable, relevant content, asking questions to encourage engagement, and responding promptly to comments and messages.

Twitter

Twitter's real-time nature means that brevity and timeliness are paramount. The platform is ideal for participating in live conversations, particularly about trending topics or industry news. With a fast-moving feed, businesses must stay current and add value to the conversations happening around them.

> **Etiquette Tip**: Avoid flooding your followers' feeds with too many tweets in a short time. Be timely with responses and interactions, and participate in trending discussions or hashtags where relevant. Always aim to provide insight or add value to the conversations happening on the platform.

LinkedIn

LinkedIn is primarily a professional platform designed for networking, career development, and B2B engagement.

Users on LinkedIn are typically looking for educational content, industry news, and professional development opportunities. As such, businesses must maintain a professional tone when engaging on this platform.

> **Etiquette Tip**: Keep your posts and comments professional. Avoid using overly casual language or sharing content that is irrelevant to the business-focused nature of LinkedIn. Ensure that your posts contribute value to your network, whether it's sharing thought leadership content, industry insights, or business achievements.

2. Tips for Maintaining Professionalism and Authenticity

Maintaining professionalism and authenticity is crucial to building long-term relationships with your audience. While social media is an opportunity to show your brand's personality, businesses must still uphold a level of decorum to protect their reputation and foster trust.

Be Transparent

Transparency is key to building trust with your audience. When it comes to business practices, product quality, or customer service, being open and honest helps establish credibility. If something goes wrong, it's essential to own up to it and address the issue with integrity rather than trying to hide it.

- **Example**: If a product falls short of customer expectations, don't ignore the problem. Acknowledge the issue, offer a solution (such as a refund or replacement), and communicate the steps you're taking to resolve it. This shows your audience that you're committed to improvement and customer satisfaction.

Avoid Over-Promotion

While promoting your products and services is necessary for business growth, over-promoting can turn followers off. Constantly pushing sales-focused content can lead to disengagement. Instead, focus on offering value through educational, entertaining, or informative content that subtly incorporates your products or services.

- **Example**: Instead of pushing hard sales posts, share customer success stories, educational articles, or industry insights. This provides followers with valuable information and builds your brand as an authority in your field.

Be Responsive

One of the most important aspects of social media etiquette is being responsive. Customers expect timely responses to their inquiries, comments, and messages. While it's unrealistic to be available 24/7, it's important to set clear expectations for response times and adhere to them.

- **How to Be Responsive**: Acknowledge customer concerns promptly, even if you can't resolve the issue immediately. A simple acknowledgment that you're looking into the problem and will follow up is often enough to demonstrate your commitment to customer service. Transparency about response times can also manage expectations and prevent frustration.

Keep It Positive

Handling negative comments or criticism with professionalism and empathy is essential to maintaining a positive brand image. Although negative feedback is inevitable, responding with kindness and offering solutions can turn a dissatisfied customer into a loyal advocate.

- **Example:** If a customer leaves negative feedback, refrain from arguing or responding in anger. Instead, empathize with their concerns, apologize if necessary, and provide a solution. For instance, if a customer complains about a late delivery, apologize for the inconvenience, explain what caused the delay (if appropriate), and offer a discount or free shipping on their next purchase to make up for it.

Conclusion

Understanding the etiquette of each social media platform and maintaining professionalism and authenticity can significantly enhance your brand's online presence. Adhering to the unique rules of each platform, being transparent and responsive, and avoiding over-promotion will help build stronger relationships with your audience. By following these social media etiquette guidelines, businesses can foster a positive, professional, and authentic brand identity that resonates with followers and encourages long-term engagement.

Crisis Management on Social Media

In the fast-paced digital landscape, a public relations crisis can emerge at any time, often catalyzed by social media. Whether it's due to a product recall, an angry customer's public complaint, or a social media blunder, how a business handles a crisis on these platforms can have a long-lasting impact on its reputation. In this section, we'll explore effective strategies for managing crises on social media, alongside how to create a comprehensive crisis management plan to navigate these situations with confidence.

1. How to Handle PR Crises and Negative Publicity

When a crisis hits, how your business responds on social media is crucial. A swift, strategic, and empathetic response can go a long way in mitigating damage and rebuilding trust. Failing to manage the crisis properly could lead to long-term brand damage, lost customers, and a tarnished reputation. Here are the essential steps in managing a social media crisis:

Acknowledge the Issue

The first and most important step in crisis management is acknowledging that something went wrong. Failing to do so or trying to cover up the issue can severely damage your credibility and trust with your audience. Acknowledging the situation shows that your brand takes responsibility and is actively working to resolve it.

- **Example**: If a product malfunction occurs, the first step should be a public acknowledgment of the problem. A statement might say, "We are aware of an issue with our product, and we are investigating the situation to ensure it is resolved as quickly as possible." This reassures customers that you're not ignoring the issue.

Be Transparent and Honest

Transparency during a crisis is critical to maintaining trust. While you may not have all the answers right away, providing your audience with the information you do know is important. Avoid making vague or evasive statements that could make the situation seem worse. Even if you're still investigating the matter, it's crucial to communicate honestly about what is happening and how you plan to address it.

- **Example**: If a food product is recalled due to a safety concern, you should immediately share what is known about the cause and any immediate steps your company is taking to ensure safety, such as halting production or conducting further testing.

Apologize When Necessary

A genuine apology is a key part of crisis communication. If your business is at fault, own the mistake and offer a heartfelt apology. Apologizing not only demonstrates empathy for your customers but also helps to diffuse frustration. However, it's important that your apology is sincere and not simply a means of appeasing your audience.

- **Example**: "We apologize for the inconvenience and frustration this has caused. We understand the impact this has on you, and we are deeply sorry for the mistake. We are taking immediate steps to rectify the situation and ensure it doesn't happen again."

Offer Solutions

After addressing the issue, shift the focus to solutions. Demonstrate that you are actively working to resolve the problem by offering practical steps to help affected customers. Whether it's offering refunds, issuing replacements, or making procedural changes, provide clear, actionable steps and make sure your audience knows how to proceed.

- **Example**: "We are offering a full refund to all customers who have been affected by this issue. Additionally, we are enhancing our quality control processes to prevent this from happening in the future."

Monitor the Situation

A crisis doesn't end once you've issued an initial statement. It's essential to monitor social media closely to track the fallout and respond to further comments, questions, or concerns. By staying engaged, you can provide ongoing updates and manage the narrative, rather than letting the situation spiral out of control.

- **Example**: Assign a dedicated team to keep an eye on social media platforms, respond to any emerging concerns, and update the audience on the status of the issue, such as when the affected products will be available again.

2. Creating a Crisis Management Plan

Having a crisis management plan in place is crucial to ensure a coordinated and effective response in times of crisis. With the right preparation, your business can act swiftly and with confidence. Here's what you should include in your plan:

Define Potential Risks

Identify the types of crises that could potentially affect your brand on social media. These may include negative reviews, product defects, service failures, social media mishaps, or employee misconduct. By anticipating possible issues, you can prepare more effectively for managing them.

- **Example**: A company might identify the risk of negative publicity from a product defect, a controversial public statement by a company executive, or a viral customer complaint.

Designate Crisis Team Members

Assign specific team members to handle crisis situations. This should include a designated spokesperson who can address the public and media, as well as a social media manager who can respond to online feedback. Ensure that each member of the team is trained in crisis communication and understands their responsibilities during a crisis.

- **Example**: A crisis communication team could consist of the PR manager, social media manager, legal advisor, and senior leadership to ensure all aspects of the crisis are addressed.

Establish Clear Guidelines for Communication

Develop clear guidelines for how your business will communicate during a crisis. This includes defining the appropriate tone (e.g., empathetic, transparent, and solution-focused), crafting key messaging points, and setting clear response times. These guidelines help ensure consistency and professionalism across all communications.

- **Example**: "In a crisis, all communication should be calm, clear, and focused on addressing the problem. Avoid using defensive language or making excuses."

Prepare Pre-Drafted Responses

While it's impossible to predict every crisis, having pre-drafted responses for common issues can save valuable time. These pre-written messages can be easily adapted to suit specific situations, allowing your team to respond quickly and efficiently when a crisis occurs.

- **Example**: A pre-drafted response for a shipping delay might read: "We apologize for the delay in shipping and are working hard to get your order to you as soon as possible. Thank you for your patience."

Evaluate and Learn from Each Crisis

After the crisis is resolved, take time to evaluate your response and the outcome. What went well? What could have been handled better? Use the lessons learned to refine your crisis management plan for future incidents. By continuously improving your response strategies, you can ensure better outcomes in the face of future challenges.

- **Example**: After managing a product recall, the team should gather feedback and analyze customer sentiment to determine if the communication was effective and if any key areas need improvement for future crises.

Conclusion

Crisis management on social media requires swift, strategic, and empathetic responses. By acknowledging the issue, being transparent, offering solutions, and maintaining close communication with your audience, you can mitigate damage and rebuild trust. Having a well-prepared crisis management plan in place ensures that your team is ready to handle any situation, protecting your brand and reputation in times of crisis. Through careful planning and thoughtful execution, businesses can turn a crisis into an opportunity for demonstrating commitment to customer satisfaction and corporate responsibility.

Mastering social media is not just about understanding the technical aspects of platforms, but also about maintaining professionalism, authenticity, and a keen sense of etiquette. By avoiding common mistakes, adhering to platform-specific etiquette, and being prepared for crises, businesses can thrive in the fast-paced world of social media. A thoughtful, consistent, and proactive approach will allow businesses to engage with their audience effectively, build stronger relationships, and navigate any challenges that arise with confidence.

Chapter 10: Social Media Content Calendar & Templates

In the fast-paced world of social media marketing, consistency is crucial. One of the best ways to ensure that you stay organized, meet deadlines, and maintain consistent messaging is by creating a comprehensive social media content calendar. A content calendar helps you plan your posts, promotions, campaigns, and engagement strategies in advance, ensuring that your social media efforts align with your business goals and resonate with your target audience. This chapter will explore the benefits of planning your content, how to build an effective content calendar, and provide templates and resources to streamline the process.

Creating a Social Media Content Calendar

A social media content calendar is a strategic tool that helps businesses plan, organize, and schedule their social media content ahead of time. By laying out a schedule for when, where, and what to post, you ensure that your content is purposeful, consistent, and aligned with your marketing objectives. Below, we will delve into the benefits of planning your content in advance and guide you through the process of building a content calendar that works for your business.

Benefits of Planning Your Content in Advance

1. **Consistency**

Regular posting is key to staying relevant and maintaining engagement with your audience. By planning your content ahead of time, you can ensure that your posts are consistent in both frequency and messaging. This consistency helps you stay on your audience's radar and keeps your brand top-of-mind, fostering a sense of reliability. Planning also allows you to maintain a balance between promotional and engaging content without overloading your audience.

2. **Time Management**

Social media can become overwhelming when you have to come up with content ideas on the spot. Planning your content in advance allows you to set aside dedicated time to focus on other aspects of your business, without the stress of scrambling for content ideas. When you have a content calendar, you can batch-create posts and schedule them for future publication, saving valuable time and energy. This also reduces the pressure to create content on the fly and enhances the quality of your posts.

3. **Goal Alignment**

A content calendar helps you ensure that every post supports your broader business goals. Whether you want to drive sales, increase brand awareness, or engage with customers, planning your content in advance makes it easier to design posts that align with your objectives. Without a content calendar, your social media efforts might become disjointed and less effective, as posts may lack focus and direction. With a calendar, you can strategically plan content around specific campaigns or initiatives.

4. Better Audience Engagement

By planning your content, you can coordinate your posts with key events, holidays, and trending topics. This proactive approach allows you to join relevant conversations and tap into events that matter to your audience. You can also tailor your content to be more engaging by using a variety of formats, such as videos, polls, and user-generated content, all within the context of your larger strategy. Furthermore, timely content—like celebrating holidays or acknowledging industry events—helps your brand seem current and connected with your audience's interests.

5. Improved Collaboration

If you have a team working on social media, a content calendar helps improve collaboration. Each team member will know what content needs to be created, when, and by whom, which helps reduce confusion and ensures a smooth workflow. A content calendar serves as a central hub for planning and provides a reference point for everyone involved in content creation. It helps in assigning tasks, ensuring that deadlines are met, and maintaining a cohesive brand message across various platforms.

How to Build a Content Calendar That Aligns with Your Goals

Building a content calendar that is effective requires strategic thinking and a thorough understanding of your business objectives. Here's how to create a content calendar that aligns with your goals:

1. Define Your Goals

Start by defining what you want to achieve with your social media efforts. Are you aiming to increase brand awareness? Drive traffic to your website? Generate leads? Boost customer engagement? Your goals will guide the type of content you create and how you schedule it. For example, if your goal is lead generation, you may focus on creating educational content and driving traffic to landing pages with strong calls to action (CTAs). Similarly, if you're aiming to increase engagement, you might prioritize interactive posts like polls or Q&As.

2. Know Your Audience

Understanding your target audience is essential when creating a content calendar. What are their interests, pain points, and challenges? When are they most active on social media? Knowing your audience allows you to tailor your content to their preferences and optimize your posting schedule. For instance, if your target audience consists primarily of young professionals, you may want to post during lunchtime or after work hours when they're more likely to be online. You can use audience insights from your social media platforms or tools like Google Analytics to help refine your posting schedule.

3. Choose Your Platforms

Not all social media platforms are created equal, and not every platform will be right for your business. Before creating your content calendar, determine which platforms are most important for your brand. For example, LinkedIn may be ideal for B2B marketing, while Instagram may be better suited for visually-driven content. Once you've identified the platforms, tailor your content to fit the platform's strengths. For instance, Instagram may require highly visual content, while Twitter may require short, punchy posts that are highly engaging.

4. Plan Content Themes

Establish content themes that align with your brand's voice and objectives. Themes help create consistency and give your audience a reason to keep coming back. Examples of content themes could include "Motivation Mondays," "Behind-the-Scenes Wednesdays," or "Feature Fridays" where you highlight customer success stories or employee features. Having clear themes for each day or week ensures that your content is varied and interesting, preventing it from becoming repetitive or stale. Themes also make it easier to come up with new ideas within a defined structure.

5. Determine Content Types

A good content calendar incorporates a variety of content types, including posts, videos, stories, polls, and infographics. Varying the content type will help maintain your audience's interest and engagement. For example, use infographics to share data, videos to provide behind-the-scenes looks, and polls to ask for feedback or opinions. Keep track of which content types perform best and optimize your strategy accordingly. Experimenting with different content types also helps you identify what resonates most with your audience.

6. Map Out Important Dates

Include important dates on your calendar that could impact your content strategy. These could include holidays, product launches, seasonal campaigns, industry events, or trending topics. By planning around these dates, you can create timely content that resonates with your audience. For example, if you're a retailer, you might plan special promotions for Black Friday, Cyber Monday, or other key shopping holidays. Similarly, if you're in the tech industry, you could align content with major tech conferences or product launches to stay relevant.

7. Create a Posting Schedule

Determine how often you will post on each platform. This schedule will depend on the platform's nature and your audience's behavior. For example, Twitter requires more frequent posting due to its fast-paced nature, while LinkedIn may require fewer posts per week but with more detailed content. Use your content calendar to schedule posts for each platform based on these insights. Additionally, consider the time of day when your audience is most active on each platform to optimize engagement.

8. Review and Adjust

A content calendar isn't set in stone. It's important to regularly review your results and adjust your calendar as needed. Monitor your engagement rates, click-through rates, and other key performance indicators (KPIs) to see what's working and what's not. Use this data to tweak your content plan and posting schedule accordingly. This allows you to stay agile and respond to trends or shifts in audience behavior.

Regularly reviewing your content calendar also helps you stay ahead of potential content gaps or missed opportunities.

By following these steps and understanding the core benefits of planning ahead, you can build a content calendar that not only helps streamline your social media efforts but also ensures that your content is aligned with your business goals and resonates with your audience.

Templates and Resources

Creating and managing a social media content calendar can be time-consuming, but using templates and tools designed for this purpose can significantly streamline the process. These resources help ensure that your content is consistent, strategic, and aligned with your brand's goals. Below are several essential templates and resources that can help you stay organized and efficient, whether you're managing one platform or multiple accounts.

Sample Templates for Social Media Posts, Ad Creatives, and Engagement Campaigns

1. **Social Media Post Template**

A social media post template standardizes your content, ensuring uniformity across platforms and posts. This helps streamline your process while maintaining consistent branding and messaging. Here's a template you can use to create engaging and effective social media posts:

- **Post Type**: (Image/Video/Story/Link/Infographic) Define what type of post you're creating. Different content types require different approaches and formats.

- **Date**: (When you plan to post) Choose a date for publication to keep your posting schedule on track.

- **Platform**: (Instagram, Twitter, Facebook, etc.) Specify which social media platform this content is intended for, as each platform has unique formatting and audience preferences.

- **Post Content**: (Write the caption or text you plan to include) Craft your message clearly, keeping it aligned with your brand voice. Include any copy you plan to publish.

- **Call to Action (CTA)**: (e.g., "Shop Now," "Learn More," "Tag a Friend") Add a compelling CTA that encourages your audience to take action.

- **Hashtags**: (Include relevant hashtags to expand reach) Select relevant, trending, and branded hashtags to increase visibility and engagement.

- **Link**: (Any URL you plan to include in the post) If you're directing followers to a webpage, include the link that supports your objective.

Using this template, you can ensure each post is structured to engage your audience, promote your brand, and drive specific actions.

2. Ad Creative Template

When planning paid advertisements, a clear and effective ad creative template is crucial for ensuring your campaigns are optimized and aligned with your business goals. Here's a template you can use for designing ad creatives:

- **Ad Objective**: (Brand Awareness, Lead Generation, Traffic, Conversions, etc.) Define the main goal of your ad to guide the creative process. This helps ensure your ad supports your overall marketing strategy.

- **Target Audience**: (Who are you targeting?) Specify the demographic and psychographic details of your audience, including age, interests, location, and behaviors.

- **Headline**: (Catchy, attention-grabbing headline) Write a concise, compelling headline that speaks directly to your target audience's needs or desires.

- **Body Text**: (Short description of the offer or message) Provide a brief explanation of what you're offering, focusing on the benefits for your audience.

- **Image/Video**: (Link or reference to the ad creative) Include a visual element (image or video) that complements your message. Ensure it's high quality and optimized for the platform.

- **CTA**: (e.g., "Sign Up Today," "Shop Now," "Learn More") Include a clear call to action that motivates the viewer to take the desired step.

By following this template, your paid ads will be clear, focused, and optimized for your goals, ensuring you get the best return on investment.

---

3. Engagement Campaign Template

To encourage user interaction, build brand loyalty, and boost community involvement, running engagement campaigns is a highly effective strategy. Below is a template to help you organize and execute successful engagement campaigns on social media:

- **Campaign Name**: (e.g., "#CustomerOfTheMonth" or "#SummerGiveaway")
  Create a catchy and memorable campaign name that reflects the campaign's purpose and encourages participation.

- **Objective**: (Increase Engagement, Build Brand Loyalty, Gain Followers)
  Clearly define the campaign's main objective to ensure you're measuring success in the right way.

- **Content Type**: (Poll, Contest, Q&A, User-Generated Content)
  Specify the type of content you will use to engage with your audience. This could be a contest, poll, or anything that encourages interaction.

- **Start Date**: (When will the campaign begin?)
  Determine the start date to ensure your team is ready to launch and that the timing aligns with your strategy.

- **End Date**: (When will the campaign end?)
  Define an end date to create a sense of urgency and give your audience a clear timeframe for participation.

- **How to Participate**: (Tagging, sharing a post, using a hashtag,   etc.) Clearly outline the steps participants need to take in order to join the campaign. Make it as easy as possible for them to participate.

- **Prize/Offer**: (If applicable, specify the reward) If there's a prize or incentive, describe what participants will receive for their engagement (e.g., a discount, gift card, free product, etc.).

- **Hashtags**:   (Campaign-specific   hashtags) Include unique hashtags for the campaign to help increase discoverability and encourage participants to use them in their posts.

By organizing and planning your engagement campaigns with this template, you can ensure they are structured, consistent, and aligned with your goals, helping you achieve higher levels of interaction with your audience.

Tools and Resources for Social Media Management

In addition to templates, there are several tools and resources available to make the process of managing your social media content calendar easier and more effective. Some popular tools include:

- **ContentCal**: An intuitive tool that allows for easy scheduling, content planning, and team collaboration. It's great for visualizing your content strategy and tracking progress.

- **Trello**: A versatile tool that can be used for managing tasks and organizing your content calendar. Trello's drag-and-drop features make it easy to visualize your content pipeline.

- **Hootsuite**: An all-in-one platform for scheduling posts, tracking engagement, and analyzing performance across multiple social media platforms.

- **Buffer**: Buffer allows for content scheduling and provides detailed analytics to track engagement and optimize your posting strategy.

- **Canva**: Canva provides user-friendly design tools to create eye-catching visuals for your social media posts, including templates for posts, stories, and ad creatives.

By using templates and these tools, you can stay organized, create effective content, and ultimately drive better results from your social media efforts.

Tools for Scheduling and Managing Your Content Calendar

Effectively managing and scheduling your social media content is crucial to maintaining a consistent online presence and ensuring that your campaigns are timely and cohesive. With the right tools, you can streamline your content planning, scheduling, and analysis, allowing you to focus more on content creation and audience engagement. Below are several powerful tools that can help you schedule and manage your content calendar more efficiently.

1. Buffer

Buffer is a popular and user-friendly scheduling tool that helps businesses and individuals manage their social media presence across multiple platforms. Buffer's simplicity and versatility make it a go-to solution for many content managers. Here's how Buffer can benefit your content calendar management:

- **Multi-Platform Scheduling**: Buffer allows you to schedule posts across different social media platforms, including Facebook, Instagram, Twitter, LinkedIn, and Pinterest. It supports both organic and paid posts, making it ideal for comprehensive content planning.

- **Analytics & Insights**: One of Buffer's standout features is its robust analytics. You can track the performance of your posts, determine which content resonates most with your audience, and adjust your content strategy accordingly. Buffer provides insights into engagement, reach, and click-through rates, helping you optimize future posts.

- **Team Collaboration**: Buffer also allows teams to collaborate seamlessly. You can assign tasks, share feedback, and manage content approvals in one central place, making it easier to stay organized.

Buffer is ideal for teams of any size, from small businesses to large enterprises, due to its intuitive interface and scalability.

2. Hootsuite

Hootsuite is another widely-used social media management tool that offers comprehensive features for scheduling, monitoring, and analyzing social media content. It's a robust platform for brands looking to improve their social media strategy and streamline their content operations. Here's what Hootsuite brings to the table:

- **Scheduling & Automation**: Hootsuite enables you to schedule posts in advance and automate your social media posting process. It supports a variety of platforms, including Facebook, Twitter, LinkedIn, and Instagram, which allows you to manage all your accounts from one place.

- **Social Listening**: Hootsuite offers social listening features, which can track brand mentions, monitor competitors, and help you stay on top of relevant conversations and trends. This is particularly valuable for understanding your audience's sentiments and discovering new content opportunities.

- **Advanced Analytics**: Hootsuite's analytics tools allow you to measure the impact of your content. The platform offers detailed reports on engagement, performance, and audience insights, helping you refine your content strategy and optimize for better results.

- **Collaborative Features**: Hootsuite's team management functionality makes it easy for multiple users to collaborate on the content calendar, delegate tasks, and review content before publishing.

Hootsuite is well-suited for businesses that require a powerful tool to manage multiple social media accounts, track performance, and engage with their audience at scale.

3. Sprout Social

Sprout Social is known for its user-friendly interface, powerful features, and robust analytics, making it a favorite among social media professionals. It's an excellent tool for businesses looking to manage their social media presence and customer support all in one platform. Here's how Sprout Social stands out:

- **Comprehensive Social Media Management**: Sprout Social allows you to schedule, publish, and analyze content across various social media platforms. You can create a detailed content calendar, plan your posts ahead of time, and ensure consistency across all your social accounts.

- **Engagement and Customer Support**: One of Sprout Social's unique features is its integrated inbox for managing customer messages. It consolidates all social media messages into one easy-to-navigate interface, helping you respond quickly to customer inquiries and comments.

- **Advanced Reporting**: Sprout Social's detailed reporting and analytics tools offer actionable insights into your social media performance. You can monitor audience growth, track engagement trends, and generate reports to help refine your content strategy.

- **Team Collaboration & Workflow**: The platform offers team collaboration features, including task assignments, content approvals, and shared calendars, allowing multiple team members to work on the same content calendar without confusion.

Sprout Social is ideal for businesses that need advanced analytics and an efficient way to manage both content and customer engagement across multiple platforms.

---

4. Trello

While Trello is not specifically designed for social media management, its visual board format makes it an excellent tool for managing your content calendar. Trello's flexibility and simplicity help you organize your content strategy in a visually appealing and easy-to-navigate way. Here's how to use Trello for social media planning:

- **Visual Content Calendar**: You can create boards for each social platform (e.g., Facebook, Instagram, Twitter) and categorize posts by type (e.g., blog posts, product promotions, engagement). Each card can represent a post, and you can add details such as post date, copy, image/video links, hashtags, and more.

- **Due Dates & Reminders**: Trello allows you to set due dates for each post, ensuring you stay on track with your content publishing schedule. You can also set reminders for upcoming posts and deadlines.

- **Team Collaboration**: If you work in a team, Trello's collaboration features let multiple team members add content, leave comments, and update the status of each post. You can also attach files, images, or links to each card.

- **Customization**: Trello is highly customizable, and you can add labels, color codes, checklists, and more to keep your content organized.

Trello is ideal for teams who need a simple, visual way to plan and track their social media content and campaigns.

---

5. Google Sheets/Excel

For businesses that prefer a straightforward, highly customizable solution, Google Sheets or Excel can serve as an effective content calendar tool. These platforms are especially useful for businesses that need flexibility and want to build a content calendar from scratch. Here's how you can use Google Sheets or Excel for content scheduling:

- **Customizable Content Calendar**: You can create a content calendar using rows for dates and columns for platforms, post types, content themes, and CTAs. This structure allows for maximum flexibility and customization based on your specific needs.

- **Collaboration**: Google Sheets offers real-time collaboration, making it easy for multiple team members to contribute to the content calendar. You can also share the document with stakeholders and get their input.

- **Tracking & Notes**: In addition to planning your posts, you can use Google Sheets or Excel to track post performance (e.g., engagement, reach, clicks) and add notes for improvements. This helps you stay organized and evaluate what works.

- **Ease of Use**: Both Google Sheets and Excel are easy to use and allow for quick edits and updates. Plus, they integrate well with other tools like Google Analytics, providing you with easy access to your data.

Google Sheets and Excel are perfect for businesses that prefer a low-cost, customizable solution and need complete control over the structure of their content calendar.

Conclusion

Using the right tool to schedule and manage your content calendar can save you time, enhance your efficiency, and help you stay organized. Whether you prefer a powerful, all-in-one platform like Buffer, Hootsuite, or Sprout Social, or a flexible, customizable option like Trello or Google Sheets, there's a tool for every business need. Select the one that fits your team's workflow, goals, and resources to ensure a streamlined and successful content strategy.

A well-organized social media content calendar is a cornerstone of a successful social media strategy. By planning your content ahead of time, aligning it with your business goals, and using the right tools and templates, you can stay organized, maximize engagement, and ensure that your messaging remains consistent and relevant. Social media is a powerful tool for building your brand, and a well-maintained content calendar will help you harness that power effectively and efficiently.

Conclusion

In the fast-paced, ever-changing world of social media marketing, success doesn't come from simply having a presence online; it requires a careful blend of strategy, creativity, and continuous effort. To stand out, you need to adopt a proactive approach that goes beyond just posting content. Whether you're building a personal brand, promoting products or services, or fostering community engagement, your social media strategy should be thoughtfully crafted and flexible enough to adapt to shifting trends. This guide has covered the key strategies and tools that will help you navigate the complex landscape of social media marketing and optimize your online presence. Let's now recap the key takeaways and explore how to maintain momentum as you continue to build and refine your social media efforts.

Recap of Key Takeaways

Social media marketing is not just about posting content but about crafting a strategy that resonates with your audience, builds relationships, and drives meaningful results. Here are the essential principles to guide your efforts:

1. **Consistency**

   o The foundation of a successful social media strategy is consistency. When you publish content regularly, you stay top-of-mind for your audience, ensuring that your brand remains visible. Consistency helps build momentum and trust, and keeps your audience engaged and anticipating your next post. Over time, this reliability strengthens your brand's presence and reputation.

2. **Authenticity**

   o Today's audience craves authenticity. They want to connect with real people, not faceless corporations. When your brand is authentic, transparent, and relatable, you create a stronger emotional connection with your audience. Show the human side of your business through behind-the-scenes content, authentic storytelling, and genuine interactions. This builds trust, cultivates loyalty, and encourages long-term engagement.

3. **Engagement**

   o Engaging with your audience is the secret sauce to turning passive followers into active community members. Social media is a two-way street. To build a loyal following, you must interact with your audience—respond to comments, engage in meaningful conversations, share user-generated content, and host interactive sessions like Q&As. Engagement fosters relationships, strengthens your community, and drives brand advocacy, which can lead to increased reach and impact.

By incorporating these principles of consistency, authenticity, and engagement into your social media marketing strategy, you'll create a stronger, more meaningful presence that goes beyond just gaining followers—it fosters long-lasting connections.

Final Thoughts on Social Media Success

As we reflect on the core components of social media success, it's important to remember that social media marketing is a dynamic and evolving field. There's no universal formula for success, and every brand's journey will look different. However, what's universal is the need for adaptability. The social media landscape is constantly changing—new platforms, trends, and tools emerge frequently, and what works today might not be effective tomorrow.

Adaptability is key to long-term success. To stay relevant and effective, you need to remain open to experimenting with new ideas, testing out different content formats (such as Stories, Reels, or live videos), exploring new platforms, and trying out different engagement tactics. The willingness to experiment not only helps you stay innovative but also provides valuable insights into what resonates with your audience. Don't be afraid to test, adjust, and learn as you go.

In addition to staying adaptable, **continuous learning** is crucial. Social media is not a one-time effort—it requires ongoing experimentation and optimization. Monitor your analytics regularly, stay informed about emerging trends, and refine your strategies based on performance data. By embracing change, you will keep your content fresh, your audience engaged, and your brand ahead of the curve.

Remember, **social media marketing is a marathon, not a sprint**. Progress takes time, and success often comes from small, consistent efforts compounded over time. The key is to stay patient, stay curious, and stay committed to your goals. By applying what you've learned in this guide, adapting to new trends, and continuously engaging with your audience, you'll be on your way to building a robust and impactful social media presence that lasts.

Next Steps to Keep Your Social Media Efforts on Track

Now that you've established a strong foundation for your social media strategy, it's time to put these lessons into action:

- **Create a content calendar** to plan and organize your posts, ensuring a consistent and strategic flow of content.

- **Monitor your social media performance** by regularly checking analytics to identify what's working and where there's room for improvement.

- **Engage consistently** with your followers and respond to comments, messages, and mentions to build stronger connections.

- **Experiment with new formats and platforms** to keep your content dynamic and fresh. Stay on top of new features on platforms like Instagram, Facebook, or TikTok to ensure you're leveraging their full potential.

- **Stay informed** about the latest trends in social media marketing to keep your strategy current and competitive.

By taking these next steps, you'll continue to improve your social media efforts and build a meaningful, lasting presence that resonates with your audience and drives results for your business.

Next Steps

The journey toward social media success doesn't end with the completion of this guide. While you now have a strong foundation to build upon, it's essential to understand that social media is a dynamic and ever-evolving field. New tools, strategies, and trends emerge regularly, and the digital landscape is always shifting. To stay ahead of the curve, you must be proactive in continuing your learning and refining your approach. Here are the next steps you can take to continue optimizing your social media strategy and advancing your skills:

1. Keep Learning

Social media marketing is a rapidly evolving discipline, and the only way to stay competitive is by continually learning. This field offers constant opportunities for growth, whether through new technologies, emerging platforms, or evolving best practices. Here are some ways you can stay ahead:

- **Subscribe to Industry Blogs**: Follow leading blogs in the social media marketing space, such as Social Media Examiner, Buffer Blog, and Sprout Social. These sources regularly publish updates on trends, new tools, and case studies that can help you stay on top of the latest industry changes.

- **Attend Webinars and Conferences**: Participating in live webinars, virtual summits, or social media conferences allows you to learn from industry experts and gain insights into cutting-edge strategies. Look for webinars hosted by platforms like Hootsuite, HubSpot, or Sprout Social to deepen your understanding of social media marketing.

- **Follow Thought Leaders**: Influential figures in social media marketing, like Neil Patel, Gary Vaynerchuk, and Mari Smith, are great sources of inspiration. By following them on social media and reading their content, you'll stay updated on new strategies and tactics.

- **Take Online Courses or Certifications**: To build your skills and credibility in social media marketing, consider enrolling in online courses or certification programs. Many platforms, like **Coursera**, **LinkedIn Learning**, and **HubSpot Academy**, offer free or paid courses that can deepen your expertise in content creation, analytics, and strategy.

By staying informed through continual learning, you'll remain at the forefront of the social media marketing landscape and be able to apply new techniques that align with your brand's goals.

2. Experiment and Optimize

Once you've implemented your social media strategy, the key to sustained success lies in continuous experimentation and optimization. The digital space is constantly changing, and your audience's preferences may evolve over time. Here's how to keep improving:

- **Test Different Content Formats**: Experiment with various content formats to see what resonates best with your audience. For example, try combining images, videos, infographics, and live streams to capture attention in different ways. Different content types appeal to different segments of your audience, so it's essential to discover what works for each.

- **Refine Your Posting Schedule**: While consistency is key, it's also crucial to assess the optimal times for posting. Use your social media analytics to track when your audience is most active and tailor your posting schedule accordingly. You may discover that certain platforms or times of day perform better than others.

- **Engage with New Tactics**: Change up your engagement tactics regularly. Whether it's running interactive polls, hosting giveaways, or engaging in more personal conversations with followers, continuously experiment with ways to foster more meaningful connections. The more you interact with your audience, the more likely they'll become loyal advocates for your brand.

- **Analyze Your Metrics**: Use the built-in analytics on platforms like Instagram, Facebook, and Twitter to track the performance of your posts. Look at metrics like engagement rates, click-through rates, and follower growth to see what strategies are working and which ones need refinement. This allows you to make data-driven decisions for further optimization.

By consistently refining your strategy and keeping track of your results, you'll ensure that your social media efforts remain effective and continue to grow over time.

---

3. Engage with Your Community

Social media is not just about broadcasting content; it's about creating a community around your brand. Building a loyal, engaged community can lead to deeper relationships and more authentic brand advocacy. Consider these strategies to engage with your audience on a deeper level:

- **Create Private Groups**: Platforms like Facebook and LinkedIn allow you to create private groups where you can build a community of like-minded individuals and businesses. These groups provide a space for discussions, collaborations, and the sharing of valuable insights. Not only does this allow you to connect with your audience more intimately, but it also strengthens your position as a trusted leader in your industry.

- **Host Community-Building Events**: Use live video or webinars to host Q&A sessions, product demos, or educational events that allow your audience to interact with you in real-time. This fosters engagement and creates a sense of belonging among your followers.

- **Encourage User-Generated Content**: Encourage your followers to share their experiences with your brand, whether it's through testimonials, reviews, or images of them using your product or service. This type of content not only amplifies your brand message but also builds trust with prospective customers.

By focusing on building and nurturing a strong community, you will foster long-term loyalty and turn your followers into passionate advocates for your brand.

4. Monitor Industry Trends

Staying competitive in the ever-changing social media space requires keeping a close eye on industry trends. By being proactive, you can quickly capitalize on emerging opportunities and avoid getting left behind. Here's how to stay on top of trends:

- **Follow Influencers and Innovators**: Social media influencers and innovators are often the first to test out new tools, platforms, and trends. Follow them to gain insights into the latest strategies and technologies. They can offer valuable perspectives on new features and platforms that you might want to incorporate into your strategy.

- **Observe Platform Changes**: Social media platforms frequently update their algorithms, features, and tools. For example, Instagram's shift towards Reels or TikTok's increasing dominance means that new features often offer ways to engage audiences more effectively. Keep an eye on changes so you can adapt your strategy as necessary.

- **Keep Tabs on Competitors**: Your competitors can be a valuable source of inspiration. Monitor their social media accounts to see what types of content they're posting and how they engage with their followers. This will not only help you understand industry standards but also highlight potential areas where you can differentiate your brand.

- **Spot Emerging Platforms**: While Facebook and Instagram remain dominant, new platforms like TikTok, Threads, or other niche networks are gaining traction. Experimenting with these emerging platforms can give you an edge and help you reach untapped audiences early on.

By consistently monitoring industry trends, you'll be able to identify new opportunities to stay creative, relevant, and ahead of the competition.

The next steps in your social media journey are all about continuous learning, experimentation, and engagement. The digital world moves quickly, and your ability to adapt to new tools, trends, and tactics will be crucial to maintaining success. Stay curious, embrace change, and keep refining your approach based on data and feedback from your audience. By doing so, you'll position yourself to achieve long-term success and foster deeper connections with your followers.

Invitation to Join a Community or Take an Online Course for Deeper Knowledge

As you continue your journey toward social media success, I encourage you to join a community of like-minded marketers, business owners, or content creators who are committed to sharing knowledge and supporting each other. There are countless online forums, Facebook groups, and professional networks where you can exchange ideas, ask questions, and learn from others' experiences. Engaging with a community not only enhances your social media knowledge but also allows you to grow your network and expand your opportunities.

If you're looking to dive deeper into social media marketing, consider enrolling in an online course that covers advanced strategies and tactics. Whether you want to learn more about content marketing, paid advertising, analytics, or building a community online, there's a course out there that can help you take your skills to the next level. Many of these courses offer practical, hands-on training and can give you the confidence to implement more complex strategies in your social media campaigns.

Some excellent platforms for online learning include:

- **HubSpot Academy**: Offers free courses on social media strategy, content creation, and marketing fundamentals.

- **Coursera**: Offers courses from top universities and companies on digital marketing, social media strategy, and more.

- EBL Training: Provides affordable courses on a wide variety of social media topics, from beginner to advanced levels.

- **LinkedIn Learning**: A great platform for professional development with a broad range of social media-related courses.

By continuing to invest in your education and staying connected with other professionals, you'll be well on your way to mastering social media and achieving long-term success for your brand.

Final Thoughts

In conclusion, social media has become one of the most powerful tools available for brands and businesses to connect with their audiences, build brand awareness, and drive meaningful results. Its vast reach and ability to foster real-time engagement make it an essential component of any marketing strategy. However, the journey to success on social media isn't instantaneous; it requires a thoughtful, strategic approach, with a focus on consistency, authenticity, and engagement.

As we've explored throughout this guide, developing a clear and effective social media strategy is crucial to achieving long-term success. It's not enough to simply post content; the key lies in crafting a plan that reflects your brand's voice, values, and mission while also resonating with your audience. When you create a strategy that is built on these core principles, you're laying the groundwork for a strong, sustainable social media presence.

Staying Adaptable and Continuously Evolving

While consistency in your posting schedule and engagement is essential, adaptability is equally important. The digital landscape evolves rapidly, and new trends, tools, and platforms emerge frequently. Staying adaptable to these changes means you can quickly pivot when necessary, ensuring that your brand remains relevant and effective. Whether it's embracing a new social media feature, exploring emerging platforms, or experimenting with different types of content, the willingness to adapt will give you the flexibility to evolve alongside your audience's preferences and expectations.

This adaptability also includes continually optimizing your social media efforts. As your brand grows and your audience engages with your content, it's vital to monitor your performance, analyze what works, and refine your strategies based on data and feedback. By embracing a cycle of constant learning, testing, and adjusting, you'll continually improve your ability to connect with your audience and drive business success.

Patience and Persistence: Social Media as a Marathon

It's crucial to remember that social media success is a marathon, not a sprint. The results you're striving for—a loyal and engaged community, increased brand awareness, and tangible business outcomes—take time to develop. Patience and persistence are key in building a meaningful and lasting presence. Your efforts will not always yield immediate rewards, but by remaining consistent, authentic, and engaged, you'll begin to see the cumulative impact of your efforts over time.

As you navigate this journey, it's important to embrace the process rather than focus solely on the end results. Social media is an evolving conversation between you and your audience. By engaging in that conversation, you build trust, deepen relationships, and create a community that values what you offer. This connection, in turn, will lead to more sustainable growth and lasting success.

Applying What You've Learned

Now that you've gathered insights into effective social media strategies, it's time to apply what you've learned. Start by revisiting your social media plan, ensuring that it reflects the principles of consistency, authenticity, and engagement. From there, focus on refining your approach based on ongoing experimentation and learning. Track your performance using analytics tools, adapt your tactics, and continue to engage with your community.

Remember, social media isn't a static effort—it's an ongoing process that requires flexibility and growth. As you implement your strategy, keep an open mind and be willing to evolve your approach as new challenges and opportunities arise.

Exploring the Possibilities

The world of social media is full of possibilities, and it's up to you to explore them. Whether you're looking to build a community of loyal followers, increase your brand's visibility, or drive more conversions, social media offers numerous avenues to achieve these goals.

So, take what you've learned, apply it to your strategy, and keep moving forward with confidence. The tools, techniques, and opportunities at your disposal are vast, and the possibilities are endless. With time, dedication, and the right strategies, you'll see your social media efforts translate into real results—building connections, expanding your reach, and driving business success in the ever-changing digital world.

Appendix

In this appendix, we will dive deeper into key elements that can further enhance your understanding and mastery of social media marketing. This includes a **glossary of social media terms, resources for further learning,** and answers to **frequently asked questions**. Whether you're a beginner or a seasoned professional, these resources will help you navigate the social media landscape with confidence and provide the tools you need to succeed.

Glossary of Social Media Terms

Understanding the language of social media is essential for effectively engaging with your audience, analyzing performance, and making informed decisions about your strategy. Below are some of the most commonly used social media terms and their definitions:

1. **Algorithm:** The set of rules and processes used by social media platforms to determine what content appears in users' feeds. Algorithms are based on user

behavior, engagement, and other factors, and they change frequently.

2. **Engagement**: Refers to any interaction between your content and your audience, including likes, comments, shares, and other forms of participation. High engagement rates indicate that your audience finds your content valuable and relevant.

3. **Reach**: The total number of unique users who have seen your post. It helps gauge the potential audience for your content.

4. **Impressions**: The number of times your content is displayed to users, regardless of whether they interact with it or not. Impressions can exceed the number of people reached if the same user views the content multiple times.

5. **CTA (Call to Action)**: A prompt that encourages your audience to take a specific action, such as "click here," "sign up," or "buy now." A strong CTA is essential for driving conversions.

6. **Hashtags**: Words or phrases preceded by the pound sign (#) that are used to categorize or tag content on platforms like Instagram and Twitter. Hashtags help users find content related to specific topics.

7. **Engagement Rate**: A metric that measures the level of interaction with your content. It's calculated by dividing the total engagement (likes, comments, shares) by the total reach or number of followers.

8. **User-Generated Content (UGC)**: Any content created by your followers or customers that relates to your brand. UGC could be in the form of photos,

videos, reviews, or testimonials that help build community and trust.

9. **Influencer Marketing**: Collaborating with influencers (individuals with a large, engaged following on social media) to promote your products or services. Influencers can help expand your reach and improve brand credibility.

10. **Paid Social**: Refers to social media advertising where businesses pay to promote their content to a broader audience. Common platforms for paid social include Facebook, Instagram, LinkedIn, and Twitter.

11. **Conversion Rate**: The percentage of users who take a desired action (e.g., signing up for a newsletter, making a purchase) after engaging with your content. High conversion rates are a sign of effective social media marketing.

12. **Social Proof**: The psychological phenomenon where people rely on the actions of others to guide their own behavior. On social media, social proof can come in the form of likes, comments, and shares, which can influence new followers' perception of your brand.

13. **Click-Through Rate (CTR)**: A metric that measures the percentage of people who click on a link in your post, ad, or email. It's an important indicator of how well your content encourages action.

14. **Stories**: Temporary, full-screen content posts that disappear after 24 hours. Stories are commonly used on platforms like Instagram, Facebook, and Snapchat to share behind-the-scenes content, promotions, or personal updates.

15. **Geo-Targeting**: A technique used to target users based on their geographic location, allowing businesses to customize their content or ads to specific locations or regions.

16. **Viral Content**: Content that spreads rapidly across the internet through sharing, often generating a significant amount of engagement and visibility in a short time. Viral content typically resonates with a wide audience and taps into current trends or emotions.

17. **Content Calendar**: A plan or schedule that outlines the content you plan to publish on social media. It helps keep your strategy organized, ensures consistency, and aligns content with your business goals.

18. **Social Media Listening**: The process of monitoring and analyzing conversations on social media to track brand mentions, trends, and customer sentiments. It helps businesses stay informed about their reputation and improve their strategies.

19. **A/B Testing**: A method of comparing two versions of a piece of content (such as an ad or post) to determine which performs better based on specific metrics (like click-through rate or engagement rate).

20. **Brand Advocacy**: When customers or followers actively support your brand by recommending it to others, writing positive reviews, or sharing content. Brand advocates are invaluable because they help generate trust and attract new customers.

Resources for Further Learning

To continue expanding your knowledge of social media marketing, the following resources—books, online courses, and blogs—will provide valuable insights and deeper learning opportunities:

Books:

1. **"Jab, Jab, Jab, Right Hook" by Gary Vaynerchuk**
   This book emphasizes the importance of context and timing in social media marketing. Vaynerchuk explains how to craft compelling content tailored to each platform's unique culture and user behavior.

2. **"Social Media Marketing Workbook" by Jason McDonald**
   This workbook is a practical guide to mastering social media marketing. It offers exercises, case studies, and step-by-step instructions to help you create effective campaigns.

3. **"The Art of Social Media" by Guy Kawasaki and Peg Fitzpatrick**
   In this book, Kawasaki and Fitzpatrick share their expert tips on creating impactful social media profiles, content, and engagement strategies. It's a great resource for anyone looking to improve their online presence.

4. **"Crushing It!" by Gary Vaynerchuk**
   In "Crushing It!", Vaynerchuk shares the stories of entrepreneurs who have successfully used social media to grow their brands. The book offers practical advice for using social media to create a business that thrives.

Online Courses:

1. **HubSpot Academy – Social Media Strategy**
   HubSpot offers free courses on a variety of topics, including social media marketing. Their Social Media Strategy course covers creating effective campaigns, measuring success, and increasing engagement.

2. **Coursera – Social Media Marketing Specialization by Northwestern University**
   This is a comprehensive online course offering in-depth instruction on social media marketing. You'll learn about creating campaigns, analyzing metrics, and crafting content for different platforms.

3. **EBL Training – Social Media Marketing Mastery**
   EBL Training offers affordable courses covering all aspects of social media marketing, from beginner to advanced. Their "Social Media Marketing Mastery" course dives into platform-specific strategies and campaign management.

4. **LinkedIn Learning – Social Media Marketing for Small Business**
   This course is perfect for small business owners looking to maximize their social media presence. It covers strategy, content creation, and optimization tips for platforms like Facebook and Instagram.

Blogs:

1. **Buffer Blog**

The Buffer Blog is a top resource for social media tips, trends, and case studies. Buffer is a popular social media management tool, and their blog offers deep insights into social media strategy and analytics.

2. **Social Media Examiner**

Social Media Examiner is one of the leading blogs for social media marketers. It provides in-depth articles, guides, and reports on the latest trends, strategies, and tools.

3. **Sprout Social Blog**

Sprout Social's blog covers a wide range of topics, from social media trends to marketing strategies and case studies. Their posts are aimed at both beginner and experienced marketers.

4. **Hootsuite Blog**

Hootsuite's blog is another excellent source for learning about social media marketing. It provides actionable tips and tutorials, along with insights on social media tools and analytics.

Frequently Asked Questions (FAQ)

Q1: How often should I post on social media?

The frequency of your posts depends on the platform and your audience. As a general rule, it's better to post consistently, whether that's once a day, a few times a week, or weekly. Experiment to find the right balance for your audience. Platforms like Instagram and Facebook perform well with regular posting (3–5 times a week), while Twitter may require more frequent posts (1–3 times per day).

Q2: How do I increase engagement on my social media posts?

To boost engagement, create content that resonates with your audience. Use interactive elements like polls, quizzes, and contests. Respond to comments and messages promptly. Posting at optimal times when your audience is active and leveraging user-generated content also helps. The key is to consistently provide value and spark conversation.

Q3: Should I focus on organic or paid social media strategies?

Both organic and paid strategies are important. Organic social media growth helps build trust and engagement over time, while paid advertising can boost visibility and drive targeted results. It's ideal to have a balanced approach—grow your audience organically, and use paid ads to complement and accelerate your reach.

Q4: What is the best platform for my business?

The best platform depends on your business type, target audience, and goals. Facebook and Instagram are great for B2C businesses, while LinkedIn is ideal for B2B marketing. Twitter is useful for real-time updates and customer service, while TikTok is great for reaching younger audiences with creative content. Focus on platforms where your audience is most active.

Q5: How do I measure social media success?

Social media success is measured using key metrics like engagement rate, reach, impressions, conversion rate, and ROI (Return on Investment). Set clear goals, track these metrics, and adjust your strategy accordingly. Tools like

Google Analytics and platform-specific insights can provide valuable data for measurement.

About the Author

David M Arnold is an entrepreneur that owns Crystal Coast HR, Crystal Coast Websites and EBL Training. With over 28 years experience in Human Resources, David has worked with small to mid-size businesses to help drive success by implementing strategies for business growth. David is also a dedicated biblical scholar and teacher with a deep passion for uncovering the mysteries of Scripture and sharing the profound truths of the Word of God. With years of study and teaching experience, David focuses on revealing the spiritual depth and relevance of the "Fellowship of the Mystery" as referenced by the Apostle Paul. His teachings invite believers to explore the richness of God's revelations, fostering a deeper connection with Christ and an enriched understanding of their own spiritual journey by "Rightly Dividing the Word of Truth".

www.ingramcontent.com/pod-product-compliance
Lightning Source LLC
Chambersburg PA
CBHW071450220526
45472CB00003B/743